Bobby Burns

shelter

One Man's Journey from Homelessness to Hope

UNIVERSITY OF ARIZONA PRESS · TUCSON

The University of Arizona Press
© 1998 Bobby Burns
All rights reserved

www.uapress.arizona.edu

Library of Congress Cataloging-in-Publication Data

Burns, Bobby, 1958–
Shelter / Bobby Burns
  p. cm.
  ISBN 0-8165-1861-0 (cloth: acid-free paper)
  ISBN 0-8165-1862-9 (pbk.: acid-free paper)
1. Burns, Bobby—1958– Diaries. 2. Homeless persons—
Arizona—Tucson—Biography. 3. Shelters for the
Homeless—Arizona—Tucson. I. Title.
  HV4506.T83 B87 1998
  362.5'092—ddc21
  [B]

Manufactured in the United States of America on acid-
free, archival-quality paper and processed chlorine free.

·   14   13   12   11   10   7   6   5   4   3   2

This book is dedicated to my late mother, Lottie Nero (1940–1979), who instilled in me the courage never to give up and always to see the human side of people.

contents

foreword

Homelessness! A starkly sobering state of affairs for most U.S. citizens. For citizens who regard access to decent, safe, and sanitary housing as akin to inalienable rights, the thought of homelessness is almost unimaginable. Yet homelessness is a circumstance that hundreds of thousands of Americans have experienced since the early 1980s. No one knows for certain exactly how many have suffered this experience, but the estimates are depressingly large.

The unexpected and dramatic growth in the numbers of homeless people during the 1980s, coupled with the increasing visibility of those living homeless as they have spilled over into the spatial preserves of other citizens, have caused homelessness to become one of the country's most pressing domestic problems. In fact, few other social problems have generated as much public concern and discussion, ranging from intense media coverage to congressional hearings to volumes of social scientific research. One of the striking characteristics of both this widespread discussion and voluminous research is that the voices of homeless people have been relatively mute in comparison to the voices of journalists and social scientists. Because of this imbalance in perspective, we know a good bit about the causes of homelessness and the characteristics of the homeless population, but we know relatively little about the experience of homelessness from the vantage point of those who are homeless.

Bobby Burns's diary constitutes a corrective to that asymmetry by providing a firsthand, up-close, intimately personal account of his experience in a shelter and on the streets of Tucson for nearly two months. Bobby's story is not particularly analytical from a social science standpoint nor is it a scintillating work of literature. It was never intended to be either. But it is highly informative in four respects. First and foremost, it provides a graphic over-the-shoulder account of the rawboned experience of homelessness. Second, it provides a striking counterpoint to the common images of homeless people as frail and disabled; indifferent to work, if not downright lazy; threatening and criminally inclined; and generally satisfied with their lowly, stigmatized, pariah-like station in life. Third, it implicitly urges caution and temperance when confronted with the temptation to think of the homeless in a stereotypic fashion. As Bobby's account reveals, his experience with homelessness contains threads of similarity—such as his ongoing battle with alcohol—with the biographies of other homeless persons, as well as threads of dissimilarity—such as his college degree and his certification as a teacher. As a consequence, neither his biography nor his experience lends itself to simple categorization or stereotyping. And fourth, Bobby's account is a story of resilience, resourcefulness, and determination—the resilience to stand up and not be totally overwhelmed and dispirited by the unimaginable experience of homelessness, the resourcefulness to find ways to survive it, and the determination to escape it by getting off the streets.

Bobby's story is an informative and gripping autobiographical account of homelessness that no doubt will provide readers with a greater understanding both of the trials and travails one must confront to make it psychologically in a shelter and on the streets, and of the difficulties one must surmount to make it off the streets.

DAVID A. SNOW
The University of Arizona
Co-author (with Leon Anderson) of
*Down on Their Luck: A Study of
Homeless Street People* (1993)

acknowledgments

The author wishes to express his gratitude to the following persons and organizations for their help and encouragement while writing this book: Dr. Christine Szuter, editor; Susan M. Knight, manuscript editor; Dr. David Snow; Dr. Howard Smith; Charles Franklin; Denita Cordalis; Edna Thompson; Vicki Goodlow; Dana Gorton; Bonnie Demorotski; Crissy Ash; Jean Ecles; David and Judy Ray; Caryl Saarinen; Kate Merek for typing (and retyping) various drafts of the manuscript; Friends of 23rd Street; Primavera Foundation; and the University of Arizona Press.

shelter diary

thursday, day 1

With a one-way ticket from Phoenix, I arrive by Greyhound bus in Tucson, Arizona, 120 miles south on Interstate 10. I have traveled throughout the world—East Africa, the Australian outback, the breathtaking island of Bermuda, the Mediterranean countries of Spain and Italy, to the pyramids of Egypt and the beaches of Thailand and Japan—but I never have taken the time to record any impressions on paper. Now it is my stay in a homeless shelter that I write about.

I am unemployed, with $210.37 in my pocket. My only possessions are a flimsy old tote bag and a small pillowcase filled with a few clothes and two pairs of worn-down dress shoes. A two-day drunk has cluttered my mind. The weather is windy and partly cloudy, my emotional equilibrium is below zero. My will is knee-high. I must somehow recapture my spirit. I am angry. Alone in a new city, I am clueless. Outside the bus terminal, a driver offers his cab for hire. I stand inert beside my belongings, without a plan for my next move. My brain races, absorbing it all. My eyes adjust to their new surroundings. I tell the cabby I'm new in town.

In my head I quickly map out a loose plan—to rent a cheap hotel room on a weekly basis. But I learn that hotel prices are not only high, the pickings are lean for those of us with very little money. A mammoth gem and mineral show has taken over the entire city and will be here for several weeks, causing hotel prices to skyrocket. Every hotel and motel room in a seven-block radius is rented. Motel 6 wants $85 a night. Even Skid Row is in on the action. My options are limited. After phoning the shelters, I find that only one has any beds open. I have ten minutes to get there or I will be back in this same spot, holding my bags and wondering where I will sleep tonight. I hire the cabby for the three-

3

mile drive from the bus terminal.

Riding through an unfamiliar city generates feelings of emptiness and anxiety—even terror. I have avoided everything about the homeless until now. The realization hits home. I am the homeless. At 9:00 P.M., the cabby drops me at a shelter called Primavera. By now my brain has stopped working altogether. This is culture shock.

I ring the bell, and a short man opens the door. He has a clipboard in his hand and asks me for my bed number and name. I remind him that I am the man who phoned ten minutes ago. He asks me for ID and escorts me to his cluttered office.

As I size up the crowded room of homeless men, my first reaction is curiosity. Men are everywhere in this warehouse-like barracks, some moving around, others resting on the metal bunkbeds in tightly packed rows. The shelter has an unpleasant scent unlike any I've smelled before. Foul body odors waft on the air. The shelter manager has a stack of papers for me to fill out, with many questions. How long have I been homeless? One day. Do I have any mental or physical handicaps? No. Am I working? No. My source of income and my highest level of education? Substitute teacher and college graduate.

He assigns me a top bunk and hands me a sheet, blanket, and thin pillow, the kind found at a cheap motel. He also hands me a sack lunch—two bologna sandwiches in a brown paper bag. I try to settle in before eating the lunch, but I can't. The shelter is overflowing with men from all walks of life: young and old, stable and unbalanced, clean and dirty. I'm overwhelmed by the activity as men mill about everywhere, like cattle in a lightning storm.

A huge, plain structure, the shelter has a single purpose: to house the homeless. The place is not meant to be fancy; it simply offers

4

me and everyone who lives here food, a roof, and a place to sleep. Shelters are not in the business to rehabilitate people. I must do this for myself.

My most recent troubles began when I was teaching fifth grade and tutoring in a public school in Phoenix, hired as a long-term substitute. During a physical confrontation with an out-of-control special-education student, I injured my lower back. Mrs. Baily had called me to her classroom to help with a student who had become violent. The school principal was not on campus, and Mrs. Baily needed someone with muscle to restrain this boy. I have muscle, but most of my weight is fat. The student was throwing over computers, screaming at the top of his lungs, and cursing at everyone in the room. He tried to stab me with a sharpened pencil as I held onto him with a tight grip. Another male teacher and I held the student down until several cops arrived, and even then this twelve-year-old wouldn't go quietly.

A few weeks later, I lent my car to a fellow teacher at noon and he never returned. Police didn't consider the car stolen because I had given him the keys. Compounding my problems, school administrators and parents had been getting on my case for my teaching methods—or lack of teaching. I was drinking more to relieve the pressures of the job, and I began experimenting with marijuana and cocaine. My excessive drinking and drug use led to being late for work, making sloppy lesson plans, and, in the end, losing the respect of the administrators and parents. They no longer thought I was committed to teaching. I wasn't asking for sympathy, but for understanding. I needed a way out.

I quit my teaching job and sought medical attention for my back pain, which had become worse. After months of therapy, the insurance carrier decided my rehabilitation was not progressing fast enough and ordered an independent medical exam. All of my benefits were terminated when the doctor wrote a report stating I was fit for work, despite a second opinion from an orthopedic physician who stated my injury was still a problem.

A low point came when I had to apply for welfare, for $160 a month when I had been making $1,800 monthly teaching. Still, I didn't want to admit to myself I had a problem with booze and drugs.

My decision to move was with the notion that all of my problems would go away in another place. I wanted a joyous, happy, and free life. I was tired of the direction in which my life was headed. Months earlier, I had had a respected teaching job, and the next thing I knew I had lost it all, including my soul. I wanted to move somewhere, to a place where I knew no one, and start a new life clean and sober. Tucson had been a place that had always intrigued me.

As I go to bed my first night at the shelter, I feel joyless and empty, not at all finding hope in this new city. My overwhelming feeling is shame. I've never faced prospects quite this meager.

friday, day 2

My whole nervous system is crippled. As my eyes gradually open wider and I become aware of my surroundings, everything seems unfamiliar and strange, like in a bad dream. I begin to wonder about the true identity of these men who move past my bunk. I paint a negative picture in my mind as I look at each one. I think I am better than these homeless men. But I know that I am not because we share the same address. We all landed here by one ill fortune or another.

Near the office window, men gather to have their laundry done. Two men almost start a fight over who was the last person in line. Shelter policy allows the first ten men in line to have their clothes washed. A client (what the homeless are called in shelters) must physically hand his laundry over the counter at 5:30 A.M. with each article of clothing listed with his name and bunk number. Like many other services, laundry is free. Word has it, the service is pretty good, meaning you get everything back. I would rather do my own laundry anyway, keeping an eye on my belongings at this point, though this is not to mock the service for those who can't afford the Laundromat.

On my first night, only four of the 111 beds at this shelter are empty. Six staff members live upstairs in semi-private rooms, with a private shower and toilet. For the clients, the shelter offers six shower stalls, six sinks, two urinals, and two toilets without doors. Although this area is cleaned each morning, the bathroom takes a beating as men converge upon it. The bathroom gives me the creeps. I'm just not used to such a lack of privacy or so many men taking care of personal hygiene so publicly. This is something I will have to accept and get used to.

At 6:00 A.M. a shelter manager announces breakfast is being served in the dining room. The 350-square-foot area includes a long serving counter and several tables and chairs crammed together with basic appliances, such as a stove, coffee urn, and other kitchen items. This morning we're having donuts, sliced oranges, cold cereal, and coffee. The donuts, I'm told, come from a major donut chain, and they're good.

After about twenty minutes, the kitchen closes. Several men volunteer to clean the barracks, kitchen, restroom, and patio.

A shelter manager announces over the PA system that the shelter bus will leave in five minutes. I join about fifty men to board a long, white bus that will make three stops. The first is the Department of Economic Security, for food stamps and general welfare. The second stop is a soup kitchen called Guadalupe's. The last stop is downtown Tucson. A client can get off the bus at any stop. The driver, a former client named Gus, is a feisty old man in his sixties who wears thick bifocals. He yells and curses at other drivers on the road.

I get off at the last stop. Downtown I can replace my lost driver's license and Social Security card, and update my teaching credentials. This process takes me all day. I get around on city buses, asking people for directions, and I have a chance to look around my new city.

My thoughts about the future are, paradoxically, bright and muddled. Despite my past and my present situation, I feel hopeful. Everything about the city, from its desert landscape to its cultural diversity, is engaging. I have a feeling I'm going to like this place.

At 5:30 P.M., I return to the shelter. Earlier I called to tell them I would not be on the shelter bus. This phone call ensures I will have a bed for the night. If you're not riding the bus, you must call the shelter before 7:00 P.M. Each client, before being allowed to enter, must give his bed number and name, which I do.

I enter the dining room, which becomes the TV room after it's cleaned every day. Shelter managers control the TV from the main office and choose which programs will be viewed. No vote is taken. I disagree with this method, but I keep my opinions to myself. Clients never argue over the programming for fear of not being able to watch the TV at all. As I enter the room, a cloud of smoke hits me. Several men are puffing away. After five minutes I can't tolerate the coughing and hacking. I'm overtaken with disbelief that I'm living in a homeless shelter, and I'm getting sadder by the minute. I chose to be here, but it eats away at my self-esteem.

I flee to the reading room and pull *The Firm* by John Grisham off the shelf, but my reading is soon interrupted by an old man. He is thin, frail, in his late sixties or seventies. His name is Tom and he leads a sedentary existence in a wheelchair. Heavy smoking has taken its toll on his lungs and overall health. His non-stop coughing and gagging can be heard across a crowded room. He sleeps near my bed, and his cough already has become a familiar sound. He struggles to speak but has trouble breathing because of his emphysema.

When he can get his words out, he tells me how another client has taken him for two packs of cigarettes. Tom seems overly angry about losing some cigarettes and a few bucks, but I later find out the guy who ripped off Tom is a noted con man who makes a habit of getting whatever he can.

Reading my book becomes virtually impossible. The conversations interfere with any concentration. Several men boast to one another about what they owned before they hit rock bottom. One man talks about how his wife won their home and cars in a divorce. Another mentions he had a successful business until a drug addiction ruled his life, and he lost everything. A third man brags about his knack for catching freight trains from state to state and claims not to have worked a steady job in years.

By now it's 9:30 P.M. I leave the room and head for my bed. The silence in the barracks strikes, leaving me with overwhelming fear. The only movement is one of the house cats creeping under beds hunting for rats. He moves in slow motion, his eyes scanning every movement. As I walk through the dim room, I feel panic-stricken. When the lights are on, the room resembles a military barracks minus the spit-polished floors and neatly made beds. What I find here now is shadowy clutter—clothes and dark, hulking bags hanging on or stashed under bunks. For many men all of their worldly possessions hang at the ends of their beds. Others less fortunate arrive in the shelter with only the shirts on their backs.

When the lights are off, the room has a ghostly feeling about it, almost like a cemetery. The air is stale, like a foot locker that hasn't been opened in months.

As I crawl into bed No. 8, I'm wondering who's really sleeping next to me—an ex-con, a murderer, a child molester, a thief, a mental misfit, or another alcoholic/addict like myself whose life has become unmanageable? I'm so exhausted, I say a quick prayer and fall asleep.

saturday, day 3

The morning routine is becoming more familiar. After breakfast, a manager announces the list of names on the morning cleanup crew. Last night I signed up for weekend cleaning. This duty allows clients not already on a day program to stay in the shelter during the daytime hours over the weekend. My chore is to clean the shelter bus, which takes me about twenty minutes.

Clients with mental or physical problems, or those who work jobs away from the shelter, are placed on the day program and can stay in seven days a week when necessary. Others must leave from 7:00 A.M. to 5:00 P.M. If such a system were not in place, some men would walk in and out all day long. An open-door policy might allow or encourage some men to just live off of the system and not look for work.

At 9:30 A.M., I shower and dress for a visit to the University of Arizona campus. The sun is bright outside and I feel invigorated. Being on a college campus brings back memories of my college days at Arizona State University. I enjoy the atmosphere, taking this time to read, relax, enjoy the solitude among college students. I take a walk around the campus and catch a baseball game, the University of Arizona Wildcat team versus alumni players. I do this though I don't particularly care for baseball—it just doesn't move fast enough for me. But I've nothing else to do today. I'd rather be watching and playing basketball, a game I prefer because of its quick pace. However, the day and setting are too perfect to pass up.

Later, I return to the shelter to find new faces in what's becoming a familiar environment. In the evening, a social worker interviews me regarding my physical condition and my mental state. These interviews are intended to help staff in placing clients in specific programs while they stay in the shelter. The social services track provides clients with short-term or long-term counseling for substance abuse and medical or mental ailments. Job Connection is a program for clients who seek work. My problems are with substance abuse and medical afflictions, and I'm beginning to believe I have some mental defect as well. I know I need help for all of my problems, but I recognize also that I need to work. I'm afraid to tell the social worker too much about myself. This interview is a more intense intake than the one given to me on my first night. The questions are more specific, and the intent is to place me in the most appropriate program. I know I need help with my addictions, and I know I'm hurting myself by not being honest. But I continue to deny my addictions and enter the Job Connection program, which will help me save my money once I find work.

After the interview, I return to the dining room to smoke a cigarette. Tom wheels into the room with one leg propelling him along. His tousled hair indicates he has been sleeping, and he's wearing a dirty shirt. He looks like someone who has spent the night in a bus station. His facial expression is dismal, as it seems to be all of the time. He takes a puff of his cigarette and begins to cough uncontrollably—an annoying deadly cough. It scares me so much that I put my cigarette out. When I smoke, I ignore that the habit will cause me medical problems later in life. I know of the risks but I continue to smoke. It's sick. Tom is living proof of what smoking does to a person. Five men watch TV, and everyone notices how badly Tom is coughing. His coughing annoys me so much that I leave the room. One of the requirements for staying in the shelter is taking a TB test. With so much coughing, contracting TB is something that worries me a lot. The air in this place can be unhealthy with so many men living under one roof.

sunday, day 4

A few bunks over, Tom snores with his covers pulled over his head. Last night he slept in his clothes, too tired or unable to take them off. He's been wearing the same clothes for the past four days.

A young man yells out that the toiletry station is now issuing soap, shaving cream, razor blades, shampoo, lotion, and toothpaste. It is a relaxed Sunday, and no one stampedes this morning. A man named Tab is issuing supplies, and he jokes as a few men receive their hygiene items. "Some men can't decipher the difference between lotion and shampoo," he says. Tab is no better than the rest of us. He tells stories about serving time in Vietnam and recovering from alcoholism. Tab says he decided to get help for his addiction. He is waiting to enter the Veterans Affairs (va) rehabilitation program. I admire his willingness to ask for help. Part of me wants to ask for help, but my denial will not let me. Until I admit I have a problem with booze and drugs, no one can help me. Tab is divorced with two kids. He looks like Crocodile Dundee—a tough guy dressed in army clothes.

At 6:00 a.m., a manager broadcasts over the PA system that breakfast is being served in the kitchen. This morning's breakfast is lumpy oatmeal, half-bananas, donuts, and coffee. Having been a cook in the navy, I find myself being critical of the food. I know this is picky, yet I find fault as if I'm paying for the food. I guess I expect too much from this place. I also know food is expensive when you're feeding over a hundred people with exceptional appetites. After breakfast, I go out to the patio for some fresh air.

The patio is a place to socialize. A man who looks like a college professor asks me for a light. He seems not to belong, out of place. He is about sixty years old and wears reading glasses on the edge of his nose. He's wearing a nicely tailored tweed jacket, pressed slacks, and is sporting a neatly trimmed beard. His mannerisms remind me of the late comedian W.C. Fields. We introduce ourselves. Maury and I immediately enjoy each other's company. He says he sells and repairs vacuum cleaners and sewing machines.

We strike up a conversation about last night's dinner. Maury calls the meal "chili beans from hell." I agree. Local churches, civic organizations, and schools bring in the food ready to serve to more than a hundred clients because the shelter is not equipped to prepare hot meals. Some of these meal teams, as they are called, have been around for years. The backbone of the shelter, they volunteer for buying, preparing, and serving breakfast and dinner.

The morning volunteers are scurrying about cleaning the barracks and restrooms. The atmosphere is subdued after the bus leaves for its morning run. Only about thirty men remain in the shelter. The lights go off at around 9:30 A.M. to save energy, and many of the men go back to bed. The morning rush is over.

I appreciate these moments when it's quiet. There are no lines for the showers or urinals. After I shower, I shave not only my face but also my entire head. I started this ritual several years ago. A haircut these days costs too much, and besides, if I'm going to be partially bald, I might as well be totally bald. I've cut myself only once, a good-size gash.

I decide to eat breakfast at a Jack-In-The-Box nearby. As I enter the restaurant, I recognize a client from the shelter sipping on some coffee. We greet each other with friendly nods and smiles. I order a 99-cent burger and a glass of water and sit a few seats away from him. Our conversation begins with my asking him about the city's bus service on Sundays. He tells me it's OK, for a Sunday. The bus heading downtown runs every half hour.

I ask about his impression of the VA hospital near the shelter, and he begins to tell me his full medical history. This guy's conversation sounds like monologue from a play that has run too long with acting that has gone stale. He admits he suffers from post-traumatic stress disorder from his service in the Vietnam War—the same illness shared by the teacher who stole my car. I immediately develop a bias against this man. Sure, the war sent back men who have this ailment and have legitimate claims. I think that many, however, are conning taxpayers out of billions of dollars.

The vet and I are joined by another man from the shelter. The vet asks the man how much money he made the day before by holding a "Will work for food" sign. "Fifty dollars," he replies. Then he tells the vet he is using the money to support his drug habit. The vet admits to the same scam. He boasts he's the greatest panhandler in town, claims to ask only for five to ten dollars at a time by studying the person he aims to target. It dawns on me this has to be the same man who took Tom for two packs of cigarettes. He's a smooth talker, good enough to con a little old lady into taking out a home mortgage.

Outside, the day is sunny. I decide to visit the University, where my first stop is the Memorial Student Union.

When I was an undergraduate at cross-state rival Arizona State University, the student union was a favorite spot of mine on campus. The union here is the same with its mini-mall atmosphere, TV lounge, movie theaters, eateries, and a variety of people around. Today I feel liberated, watching TV in this quiet room by myself—fresh air and not a soul in sight. Men in the shelter seem to shudder at educational programming on TV. I'm free to watch the programs I like here and avoid those I don't care for. I prefer educational programs such as documentaries, nature shows, true drama, and sports. Another amenity that brings me some comfort is the clean restroom in the Union, a welcome change after having to use the shelter restroom.

Visiting the University makes me feel like I belong, and this feeling means a world of difference to my overall state of mind. It gives me a chance to focus on my thoughts away from the often-dismal environment of shelter life. I become overwhelmed with negative thoughts and hopelessness if I sit around the shelter all day. Escaping to the University is a reminder that I haven't always been down on my luck.

In the early afternoon I board a trolley for a ride to the Fourth Avenue district of town, where the 1960s meet the 1990s in Tucson. One finds a little of everything—a health food cooperative, thrift stores, antique shops, bike shops, classical bookstores, panhandlers, bars, and restaurants offering foods from the Southwest and Central America. It's an area that attracts people from all over the city and from all walks of life.

Today I notice a man who lives at the shelter sitting near a western clothing store, drinking carrot juice. He's middle-aged and wears thick glasses. He is clean-shaven, wears clean clothes. Everything on his backpack, from his sleeping bag to his cooking pans, looks as though it has never been used. Something is odd about this picture, but I can't put my finger on it. I approach the man with a sense of caution and apprehension. His body language indicates he does not wish to interact with people, as though he has built a wall around himself, warning others to keep their distance. I get the impression he's paranoid.

We recognize one another and exchange names. He tells me he's from New England. We speak for about five minutes, then he abruptly puts his backpack on his shoulders and says good-bye. When I offer to shake his hand, he refuses point blank.

My day has been full. I return to the shelter. While I'm reading my book, the dinner line is long and ends near my bunk. Two men are talking, and one says to me, "I have nineteen children by three different women, and this is my youngest." Imagine! A father and son being together in a shelter.

The father is in bad shape. His face is badly swollen, and both of his eyes are blackened. He talks with a Texas accent. His son is a handsome fellow. They tell me they've been in a terrible car accident. The story seems odd: The father went through the front windshield even though he was wearing his seat belt, and the son did not have on a seat belt and received only a scratch or two. Both men say they are lucky to have survived and have only God to thank. A shelter manager announces over the PA system that dinner will be delayed for thirty minutes. Everyone in line stays put. A few men seem bewildered, but most take the news without reaction.

A young man named Mohammed who suffers from manic depression, or bipolar disorder, has just invaded my space. He's in his mid-thirties, frisky as a filly. The guy is currently taking four different types of medication to control his illness—his eyes are bulging and his hands are shaking uncontrollably as he talks nonstop. He talks about how he loves volunteering at the VA hospital. Mohammed is waiting to receive benefits and enter the VA substance-abuse program.

Our conversation turns to a Gulf War vet he works with who is badly burned and has lost his right hand and right ear. Mohammed claims the vet is not bitter about his injuries and would do it all again. The story is a sad one. I feel lucky that I never experienced war while in the navy. I love America, but I'll take peacetime over war any day. Wars don't ever solve anything but just bring cataclysmic outcomes.

Finally, dinner is served. It's a good one tonight: chili beans, coleslaw, ham sandwiches, and fruit punch. I get the feeling each time I walk through the serving line that the volunteers who cook and prepare meals feel sorry for us. Some men actually play on this sympathy by not looking the volunteers in the eye. I can understand their shame in living in a homeless shelter, but I just go about my business, appearing to be content and just fine. Inside I feel embarrassed and it hurts. I hide my emotions so they won't see. Some stare at us, mystified. They probably think we're all loose cannons.

During dinner I sit next to the man who went through a car windshield. Next to us sits a man wearing a cowboy hat. An experienced drinker myself, I know this man smells like booze. Yet he works hard to conceal his drunkenness to avoid being caught by a shelter manager. Some drunks are adept at hiding their drunkenness. Others utter a few words and that's all it takes.

Out of the blue, the drunk man begins talking about how a person can hire a prostitute in Mexico at the Nogales, Arizona, border for ten dollars. In the next breath, he denies ever doing it. Then he seems to regret ever bringing up the subject at all. The man seems embittered, in some kind of pain. He asks me if I want his partially chewed ham sandwich, which I politely decline. I need some air, so I go to the patio to pollute my lungs once again.

The kitchen closes at 7:00 P.M. I decide to read in the reading room, which also has the misnomer of "library." The reading selection comprises mainly a few novels, Bibles, magazines, newspapers, and back issues of the *Christian Science Monitor.*

Ten people in the tiny room would create a fire hazard. Crammed into about two hundred square feet are three tables, a desk, and an ironing board and iron. Social workers conduct client intakes in this room. People gossip. Men play chess, cards, and dominoes. I've realized the best time to write or read in this room is at night. I'm disappointed that this library lacks reference books: dictionaries, self-help books, résumé-writing books, books on writing business letters, or law books. I am certain I am not alone in this concern. But who am I? People here know me as another homeless man just passing through, who will leave one day and make way for the next man. I must somehow make it through this mess I've created. I can't change the system, but I can make the best of my stay.

tuesday, day 6

I wake up at 5:00 A.M. and head to the restroom for a bird bath, a splash here and a splash there. I'm the fourth person in line to have my laundry done. There is no orderly line. We just gather around the front desk. At 5:30 A.M., a blinder opens and a shelter manager takes our pillow cases of dirty laundry.

Last night, I put my name on the morning cleanup list. My responsibility is to sweep, mop, empty trash, and clean the toilet in the office. I grab a broom and sweep the floor and complete the rest of my chores. After hearing me clean and flush the toilet, the manager comments that the resident feline forgot to flush the toilet. Supposedly, this is a true story. The cat Midnight somehow positions herself on the toilet without falling in as she takes care of her business.

The shelter has two cats. Both are given food and a warm place to sleep. Neither cat likes the other. Midnight enjoys the company of anyone who takes the time to stroke her thick black coat. The other cat, Rambo, is the son of Midnight. Rambo is a rebel of sorts. He's been known to give chase to jackrabbits and challenge rattlesnakes or dogs for the thrill of it. Rumor has it that the only reason both cats are around is to keep the rat population down. Personally, I haven't seen any rats nor do I wish to encounter them. I have no problem with the cats taking care of this small chore.

Today I will apply for food stamps for the first time in my life. I arrive at the office at 7:00 A.M., and once the office opens I complete the long application and wait to be called. I feel like I am begging, like a bum off a street corner. The individuals working in this agency treat everyone the same—coldly and impersonally. I sense they see all homeless persons as lazy. I feel angry, humiliated, and ashamed. But as with any agency like this, they have what we need, and we must endure the situation. Long waits are typical in a food stamp office. I wonder if food stamps will bring me a sense of empowerment at the grocery store, being able to buy the things I like in the way of snacks.

Finally, after two hours, my name is called. A young clerk interviews me as she intently reviews my application. She asks me several questions with a bit of a holier-than-thou attitude, then tells me I qualify for $118 in food stamps each month. In two days, I will receive emergency food stamps worth $65. Being homeless has a few perks.

My next stop for the day is the city's Special Services/Transportation offices for a reduced-rate bus card. Getting around any city requires transportation, and I must rely on city buses. Again I sense a cold and insensitive attitude. Many social service agency personnel show little respect or compassion for people who happen to be without an address. Homelessness to me means that I have no home at the moment. It's not a disease a person can catch by simply coming into contact with me.

Before I became homeless, I never took the time to think about or understand who became homeless. I looked through them. What I did know about the homeless I learned from the rhetoric put out by the media or from what I saw with my own eyes. My impression was that their predicament had to be their own fault. Homelessness was their problem, it wasn't mine—until I became part of that population. Now I realize people become homeless for countless reasons. They're not all thugs and bums; some are people who've just fallen on bad times. It seems people get concerned about helping the homeless around the holidays in November and December; they tend to forget the rest of the year. I've learned that homelessness is the same year-round, with some individuals remaining homeless for many years.

The county Health Department is my next stop, for my TB test. The exam takes less than five minutes, though I must wait a few days for the results. For once, I'm treated like a human being—at this agency.

Today has been a busy one, and I feel good about what I'm accomplishing. I'm off again, this time to the state Board of Education to have my teaching certificate validated for Pima County. I find myself having to go up and down three different elevators, go to five different buildings, speak to ten people for directions, lose ten pounds—but I finally locate the right office in some obscure room. By now I'm tired and a bit ticked. But I survive and am able to update my certificate so that I can apply for a part-time teaching position.

My final stop of the day is the VA hospital to seek help for my ailing back and to make arrangements to have my medical records transferred from Phoenix. I enter a large reception area overflowing with vets. While waiting to be called, an elderly couple quiz each other on presidential trivia. Which two former first ladies divorced twice? My name is called before I hear the answer, and I have to report to a nurse's station. It's now 4:00 P.M., and a nurse takes my blood pressure and vital signs. She looks at her watch as she says it's getting late but asks if I want to see a doctor today. I tell her I think tomorrow will be better.

I arrive back at the shelter after grabbing a quick bite of Mexican food nearby. A manager meets me at the front door after I ring the door bell and, as always, asks for my name and bunk number before allowing me to enter, a ritual that I'm becoming accustomed to but still find alienating. I change into more comfortable clothes and head to the patio to unwind.

The sun is setting as I sit atop a picnic table and reflect on my day. Then I notice what appear to be two clients hiding in a dark corner using drugs. I'm not sure what they're using, but it's not pot because I would have recognized the smell. Drugs and alcohol are common in this shelter, but you learn to mind your own business. I have smelled pot at night on the patio. A few nights ago two men were shooting heroin into their veins after the lights went out in the barracks. The restroom and patio are popular spots for sneaking alcohol and drugs. Managers make rounds, but drunks and addicts always find ways to use. I know the culture firsthand. I started drinking when I was eighteen years old. I grew up around substance abuse. My mother died from liver disease. My stepfather overdosed on drugs. My younger brother was killed in a drug deal gone bad. And I have lost my job and landed in a homeless shelter.

Each evening the shelter is abuzz. Appointments are made for doctors. Medications are handed out. New clients are told about shelter rules. Clients need stamps to mail letters. Often a man can be seen pacing up and down the hall. The two cats fight over territory. The same commotion happens every evening. The manager on duty must direct all of this activity like a cop directs traffic. He will talk into the PA system dozens of times between 7:00 to 9:00 P.M. The squawk box goes off every minute. This evening I try to read, but the hubbub overwhelms me. I wait for the lights to go off and welcome sleep.

wednesday, day 7

I awake craving a donut, so I leave the shelter and head for the donut shop. As I enter, I notice Maury sitting at the counter drinking his coffee. As usual, he is neatly dressed in a sports jacket with a white polo shirt, gray slacks, and reading glasses perched on the edge of his nose. He is sitting with another man from the shelter discussing water purifiers. I think it's the salesman in him—any chance to peddle.

After drinking my coffee, I make the short walk to the VA hospital for my doctor's appointment. I check in and am asked to have a seat in the lobby. Soon, a nurse calls me to her station and takes my pulse and vital signs. I wait again in the lobby for about twenty minutes before my name is called by a nurse practitioner, who examines me and then leaves the room to consult with a physician. The nurse comes back and advises me to take two anti-inflammatory pills and recommends physical therapy for my back pain.

On my way out, I run into Tab, the toiletry man, and we agree to have lunch in the hospital cafeteria. Tab mentions the benefits of attending Alcoholics Anonymous meetings and how his life has changed.

"I'm able to think with a clear mind today. Before, I was too drunk to do normal things, such as being with my kids sober, and this means a great deal to me today," he says.

I want to ask him more about AA, and yet I feel this is not the time. I don't yet feel comfortable discussing my alcoholism and drug use. Deep inside I want to tell my story, yet I cannot. Shame.

The lunch is quick and we both acknowledge we must get going. I catch a bus downtown. Pain begins to intensify in my lower back once I arrive at the bus terminal. I decide to rest on a bus bench a few minutes and take the weight off my back.

A lady wearing a dirty white dress and bells tied to her shoes walks up and asks me for a cigarette. She begins talking about her life in a homeless camp.

"Where is the camp?" I ask.

"It's on 'A' Mountain. Many homeless people live there."

"A" Mountain is a landmark not far from downtown Tucson. Near the top a huge white letter "A" is painted on rocks. I can only imagine what it's like for her, living in the desert with blowing dust, temperatures above the century mark, and rattlesnakes that are part of the landscape.

The young woman says she has been unable to qualify for welfare because of her mental disorders. It's obvious to me something is wrong with her. She seems unsteady on her feet, as well as mentally disturbed. Her conversation is muddled, and she seems agitated and pained.

My back is feeling better. I remember I must mail a postcard to my older brother in Phoenix. The message I write is that I haven't been drunk in six days. He, too, is an alcoholic, a drunk who has blackouts, a drunk who is stubborn when told he has a drinking problem. I lived with my brother before moving to Tucson, and it was not the best of times. Two drunks under one roof is not an ideal living situation. His blackouts were a nightmare. He'd start fights and become belligerent with me and anyone else around. He went on 72-hour drinking binges, going to any lengths to get a drink. If booze was around, he would not stop until it was all gone. Once he almost killed himself when a forklift he was operating at work fell over. He was drunk. Another time, he and a nephew nearly drove off a cliff on a narrow mountain road. They both escaped death by inches. A tow truck had to peel the car from a large rock, which had saved them from tumbling farther. Again, booze was to blame.

As I am walking downtown, I recognize another familiar face from the shelter. Lamar is doing some city work on a streetlight pole. He looks like a football player, a lineman standing about six foot, three inches and weighing 250 pounds. A bandanna covers his head in the hot sun. The day is gorgeous—eighty degrees, but his fair skin has turned lobster red.

Lamar tells me he is a recovering alcoholic and drug addict. Once again, I hear a person express gratitude for what AA has done for him. Lamar moved to Tucson, homeless, from the South. He attends three to four meetings a day. "Meetings help me to stay sober, being around new friends who share the disease of alcoholism," he says. His move to Tucson was to get away from people who drank. His optimism and attitude about sobriety are encouraging to me as I try to understand my problems with alcohol and drugs. Lamar's long-term goal is to become a full-time employee for the City of Tucson's Public Works Department. For now, he and four other shelter clients work for a city-sponsored grant program painting over graffiti.

At about 4:00 P.M. I say good-bye to Lamar and walk over to the public library to do research on the area school districts. I want to know such things as demographics, pay, school sizes, and funding for each district.

I find vital information from old newspaper clippings. I am amazed by the size of the Tucson Unified School District (TUSD), which has more than one hundred schools. The Flowing Wells School District is much smaller, comprising one high school, one middle school, and two elementary schools. TUSD sounds like a shoo-in for steady work as a substitute.

While reading over clips at the library, I recognize many faces from the shelter. Some men use the library for reading, but I suspect many more use the library for refuge from the heat and to rest their tired legs. I had assumed all homeless people were illiterate, but I'm finding many homeless people don't fit the stereotype. We're not empty, but have feelings, emotions, desires, hopes, dreams, a need to be loved, and the wish to be respected by society. I view this chapter in my life as only temporary, but I know others will follow in my footsteps when I am no longer homeless.

Maury is waiting at the bus stop. He's dressed neatly, as usual. We share experiences from the day. Within five minutes, our bus arrives for the ride back to the shelter. On the way, I suggest we go for dinner at Church's Fried Chicken. At the shelter, some dinners are better than others, and today we'd rather not leave a good meal to chance. We each order a three-piece chicken dinner special with the works: mashed potatoes with gravy, coleslaw, soft roll, and a soft drink for $2.99 plus tax.

Maury is his usual good-natured self. He hates politics passionately but loves to make fun of everything. Like any good salesman, he's a smooth talker and easy to listen to. He mentions little about his personal background or how he came to be homeless. Older men seem to have a difficult time discussing their homelessness. The reverse is true with younger clients. They seem to share more willingly about themselves and their past. But like all people, homeless men tell you just what they want you to hear.

Maury and I catch a city bus for the three-block ride back to the shelter. We are greeted at the door, asked the usual questions, and allowed inside.

Earlier in the morning a few men saw me shaving my head. An African American asked me to close-cut his hair. We agreed on a price of $1.50. Asking any more would have been greed on my part. The shelter has a barber's chair next to the toiletry closet. Volunteers come weekly to cut hair for free. I get permission to use the chair. Shortly after I start cutting, three other black men gather around wanting their hair cut. I treat this new-found vocation as sport. But I don't tell my customers I have never cut anyone's hair but my own. Besides, it's only pocket change; cutting hair is not what I had in mind when I came here.

Until now all of my victims want close-shaved cuts. Then a white guy wants a haircut. My future as a barber will be tested on this one haircut. Something tells me to be up front with this guy before I begin experimenting on his long curly hair. I bring up every excuse as to why I don't feel comfortable cutting his hair. I have never cut a white person's hair before in my life. He would be better off waiting for a more experienced barber. But this guy insists that I give it a try. He wants a designer cut—a little off the top and both sides trimmed. I trim the top without any problems, but I leave gaps so huge the poor man wants his money back. I have no problem returning his money. He'll think long about the mistake he just made, wear a hat for a few days. The double takes from other clients later become so bad that he eventually moves out. I vow not to cut any more hair but my own.

It's getting late. I grab my book and sit down to read a few chapters. Five men are in the reading room. Two are reading and the other three play cards. The room is quiet. For once, I get a chance to read in peace. Life has been good today, and I've gone another day without a drink.

thursday, day 8

This morning I have office cleanup. By now I start to learn the names of the shelter managers. Jon is on duty this morning. For the past few days I have noticed this guy's rotten attitude toward the men. Jon is as ruthless as a Gestapo thug. He's negative, disrespectful, demeaning, and an arrogant SOB. Even his co-workers grow tired of his BS. The men avoid contact with him out of fear of saying the wrong thing. Jon was recently a client in the shelter and is now a manager. How quickly one forgets! This guy takes his new-found power to extremes.

For the past three days, I have requested a lower bunk because of my back. Each time Jon has denied my request. "I don't issue bed reassignments," he says.

I don't mind being told I can't have something, but his tone bothers me. He speaks with disrespect, as if I were some piece of trash. He gives no reason why I can't change beds. I'm a patient person, but he's pushed my buttons.

Finally, after a shift change, another shelter manager assigns me a lower bunk. Directly next to me now is Tom, the old man in the wheelchair. Tom is as helpless as an infant. How he ended up in a shelter no one knows. He really should be in a nursing home. He needs help with eating, changing clothes, and bathing. His health is terrible. Now I must sleep next to him and endure his marathon coughing sessions and his nights of talking in his sleep. The price for a lower bunk.

I leave the shelter and catch a bus to the main offices of Primavera. The old building once served as an apartment complex called the Alamo Apartments. My business today is to join Job Connection, a program started in 1987 to help the homeless learn job skills, save money, and move into their own housing. My appointment is at 9:00 A.M. with Ivan, the coordinator.

Ivan informs me that the wait will be a few minutes and indicates a seat in the workroom next to his office. The workroom is small, a comfortable studio with newspaper pages of want ads spread out on a wobbly table. A rotary telephone and several phone books fill up the rest of the table. I decide to check my mail quickly at the Relief and Referral (R & R) office. Clients can receive their mail at R & R. Many of the homeless who live on the streets stop by R & R to pick up mail, use the phone, have counseling services, and freshen up. When I enter the room, several men and women occupy the chairs. A volunteer hands out condoms to a man who has had one too many to drink and has trouble keeping his balance. The man is wearing a shirt that clings to him like old gum under a school desk.

I return to Ivan's office for our meeting, which will lay the ground-work for his program.

My perception of Ivan is that he is condescending, rude, and arro-gant. He talks down to me and another man, and I get the impres-sion he's only half present and his heart isn't in his work. However, he deals with guys like me every day. And who am I? Just another homeless man passing through his doors who says he is trying to find a job. The types of individuals he encounters range from high-ly employable to those with few or no skills.

Job Connection provides two options to homeless men. A two-week program is for people just passing through town who want to earn enough money to move on. Most jobs pay daily—better known as day labor. One day you might be shoveling up someone's sewer pipes, another day you might be hauling trash to a garbage dump for eight hours for minimum wage. This Job Connection program places no restrictions on clients except that their stay in the shelter is up after two weeks.

The other program, for four to eight weeks, has strings attached. The sooner one finds work, the better. The program offers a résumé service, job skills training, and a message phone. Ivan makes it clear that if I'm not working a full-time job in four weeks, I'm out of the program. If I find work, I can have an additional four weeks in the program.

Each pay day, every client in the program must place 75 percent of his wages in savings, and he can use the remainder any way he wants. Each person is responsible for getting a money order in his name and handing it over to Ivan. Earnings are returned at the end of the program. A person can get ahead and land back on his feet if he sticks to the plan. I believe I can if I don't drink. I have no excuse not to succeed. My meals and rent are free. Finding a job seems a minor concern. I agree to the terms of the contract and sign on the dotted line.

My next priority is to go back to the county Health Department for my TB results. A nurse looks at my left arm and says my test is negative. She hands me a card showing that I am TB-free, which I will have to show the shelter. It's 11:30 A.M. and I decide to eat lunch at a downtown greasy spoon. I order a bowl of soup, a half-sandwich of tuna, and a cold glass of iced tea. I sit on the café patio as the lunch crowd comes and goes. The weather is sunny and breezy.

I later return to the R & R office to see if my food stamps have arrived. A volunteer hands me my mail. A letter from the Arizona Department of Economic Security informs me that I will receive my food stamps within five days. Leaving the office, I see a man trying to sell his food stamps to another man for cash. This sort of thing happens all the time. With cash you have more latitude. With food stamps you face certain restrictions. I walk downtown pondering what I should be doing with myself. Idle time is what gets me in trouble with booze and drugs, this I know.

Time has gone by fast today. I walk a few blocks from downtown to catch the shelter bus. As I approach the pickup point, I notice about twenty men waiting for the bus, some men I have never seen before. A few are talking, and the rest stand in silence as if they have nothing in common with one another. The bus ride is mellow as the big white bus passes through the downtown.

Uncertainty enters my mind as I size up the other men, who look as unsure and wary as I. As the bus arrives at the shelter, a manager waits at the front door with a clipboard in his hand. "Report to the second door on your right if it's your first time in the shelter," he yells.

Those of us who already have beds give our names and bunk numbers by rote. All of my possessions are shuffled onto and under my bed. I feel discouraged as I look around the cluttered barracks. Homelessness is undeniable. Still, I have problems in accepting that I have fallen this low. The oppressive environment on a daily basis, the day-to-day grind, gets to me. Every day I face the constant noise, the bothersome loudspeaker, the rules, the schedule, strange people in and out. But if I can put up with navy boot camp, then I can put up with the shelter.

friday, day 9

I awake in a cold sweat. I'm dreaming, I think. But I quickly realize my street address remains 200 East Benson Highway, a shelter for men like myself who have hit rock bottom. The morning routine goes as usual. I thank God for giving me another chance to improve my life.

After breakfast, I catch a bus to the Job Connection office to update my résumé. Ivan informs me today is not a good time for him to help me and asks me to come by tomorrow. I leave his office frustrated but not defeated. My agenda today is to fill out as many job applications as humanly possible. I travel by bus north and south, east and west, losing count of the buses caught and missed. I leave my application in the personnel offices at three school districts. I even look through the newspaper classified-advertising sections and other job announcements. The pressure to produce is making me uneasy. I have to find a job soon. I feel like I have something to prove to Ivan—that I'm not someone who waits for a job to fall in my lap. By mid-afternoon I am physically and emotionally exhausted.

I make my way to the bus terminal, where I run into a young client I recognize. He seems too youthful to be living in the shelter. As he approaches me, he hesitates, then introduces himself as James, and begins telling me about himself and a scam he's involved in.

"What I do is steal money from parking structures where customers have to put money in numbered slots," he says. These places have no lot attendants, James explains. He shows me the piece of wire he uses to slide the bills up toward a small opening. When the bill reaches the top, he uses a small pair of tweezers to pull the money out. "Today I made thirty dollars," he claims.

"How long have you been doing this scam?" I ask.

James says nothing and nervously shakes his head. Then he suddenly says he has to go. He must think I'm an undercover cop.

He also has told me a lot of personal information, that he was recently accused of attempted murder in Phoenix and has served time in prison. He is a small guy, standing about five feet, six inches and weighing about 130 pounds.

Sociologists label behavior such as James's as deviant. Our society seems plagued with this sort of behavior, especially among the poor. My drinking and drug use has not led me to commit a serious crime or land me in prison. But it has caused me problems with relationships, my health, jobs, isolation, poor self-esteem, hopelessness, and indirection.

Later I go to check my mail. Every day a printout is posted on the office door, listing from A to Z the names of everyone who has received mail. Today I find my name on the list, and I discover I've been issued $65 worth of food stamps. Before I'm out the door, a man asks if I'd be willing to sell them, and I refuse. Instead I head to the supermarket. I remember not to buy anything that needs to be refrigerated. A T-bone steak would be nice, but I have no way to cook the damn thing. I have a penchant for eating sunflower seeds, so I purchase the biggest bag I can find. I also buy fruit juices, microwaveable foods, and soups. The last item I purchase is a bottle of hot sauce. Most of the men in the shelter have their personal bottles of hot sauce at each meal.

Back at the shelter, new arrivals are given the standard intake interview, sometimes administered by college students or retired people. This evening, I eavesdrop to find how and why these men became homeless. Moreover, I want to find out how much we have in common. The intakes are held in the library, which gives some semblance of privacy. But most clients don't object that others are nearby reading or writing. I pretend to write a letter, but I'm actually taking notes about interviews, much like someone undercover.

I have always wanted to write but have never taken it seriously. I remember a navy recruiter asking me what I'd like to do in the service, and I replied that my goal was "to become a journalist." The recruiter said, "Not with these scores, pal." My second choice was culinary arts, so I later attended a Contra Costa Community College culinary arts program, and under the guidance of an Austrian chef, I learned to cook for officers aboard ships. After ten years in the food and beverage industry, I quit. I still sometimes have visions of someday owning my own café—but I have never lost the urge to write.

Tonight's intake interviews are done by an intern who is studying for her degree in social work. She is interviewing the man who says he has nineteen children and whose youngest is also living in the shelter. This man's face has numerous cuts, and he has a broken collarbone and broken ribs. He explains to the intern how he suffered the injuries when he and his son were run off the road by a semi-tractor trailer while driving from Texas. The man tells her that although he was wearing his seat belt, he went through the windshield of his late-model Cadillac. His son, though he was not wearing a seat belt, didn't receive a scratch. After several weeks in the VA hospital, he landed at Primavera.

It's late, and I want to stop writing and switch to reading more of *The Firm*, then call it a day. Lying in bed, I feel skeptical about my future. I have not found any work. I can't see myself living my life in shelters year-round like many homeless do. For some men this is the only option. Many of them work in dead-end jobs that provide barely enough to live on. Affordable housing remains a critical concern for the homeless. I fall asleep feeling alone, wishing for my circumstances to be different.

saturday, day 10

I get a late start today. The last men are leaving to catch the shelter bus when I wake up. The reading room is quiet, and I spend all morning filling out job applications. Over the PA system comes an announcement to sign up for Arizona Health Care Cost Containment System AHCCCS, a state health plan that offers medical and dental care for low-income people. I rush to place my name on the list. Later an AHCCCS worker calls me to the office and takes down information. She asks me how much money I earned last year, then she tells me I don't qualify because I made too much in the last quarter. I thought for sure I would qualify, living in a homeless shelter and being unemployed.

I've been having problems with my vision. At night, I can't see things very well at a distance. Later, a man tells me the Lions Club will help me get glasses. An issue that always confronts the homeless is what to do if we need some medical assistance. Many, like me, fall through the cracks. My VA benefits only cover my back ailment. Substitute teaching offers no health benefits, except workman's compensation for treatment of injuries received on the job. Health care in America is in a sad state when an injury or illness can send working families into financial ruin—and homelessness.

Health care hasn't changed much for the poor since 1958, the year I was born in a county hospital. My mother couldn't afford prenatal care for me and my seven brothers and two sisters. My real father was no help; I never knew him. A stepfather came into my life when I was nine. If it hadn't been for welfare and other services such as low-income housing, reduced-price school lunch programs, county health care, and other government assistance, we would not have survived.

The day at the shelter passes. Dinner is being served in the kitchen. Tonight's menu includes cold cuts (bologna, salami, and American cheese), tossed green salad, whole oranges, soft sugar cookies, and coffee. Most men eat fast to get in line for seconds and thirds. You would think they haven't eaten in days. But then, this may be the case for some of them.

During dinner, to everyone's astonishment, a message comes over the PA system that someone left a pile of human waste on the restroom floor. Everyone begins to laugh. I am dumbfounded. Why? The stalls are operational. "Will the person who did this come and clean it up," says an angry Jon, the manager on duty. No one comes forward. Whoever did this probably was upset at Jon and wanted to get back at him for something he had said or done. Jon, in the end, cleaned up the mess.

sunday, day 11

I feel as idle as the air in the barracks. Sundays are too quiet in this place. People move in slow motion, including myself. All of a sudden, it's as if a spirit comes over me to attend church. I'm not a religious zealot, but God has been good to me, even in my homelessness.

At 11:00 A.M., I catch a bus near Primavera's office to attend Prince Chapel African Methodist Episcopal. When I enter the church, my feelings of boredom and depression subside. The congregation seems friendly, as in most churches in America. Today the church is celebrating African American women in history. The pastor is a huge man who reminds me of the father on the TV show *Fresh Prince of Bel Air*. His oratory style is dramatic, and his energetic delivery and monstrous hands leave me in awe. His voice fills the sanctuary like nothing I have heard before.

African Methodist Episcopal (AME) churches have large memberships, which tend to include many professionals, from school principals to lawyers and doctors. When I was in college in Phoenix in the late 1980s, I attended an AME church with congregation members who were city councilmen, judges, educators, and working people. I remember I enjoyed singing in the church choir with a passion.

After church, I return to the shelter, which now resembles a ghost town. I enjoy the peacefulness and the solitude, but it never seems to last very long. As the sun sets an hour later, all hell breaks loose—strangers coming and going, some men trying to hide their drunkenness, managers blasting messages over the PA system. I begin to wonder if I can continue to endure all of this until I'm back on my feet.

I feel like I'm in the middle of rush-hour traffic. I try to continue reading but I'm interrupted by Mohammed, the manic-depressive. He is on several medications prescribed by a physician, including divalproex, lithium, trazodone, amantadine, folic acid, and thiamine. I don't understand how this guy takes all of this medication and admits to doing street drugs as well. Mohammed is about thirty-five years old, yet he looks older. He appears normal; but inside, he is a very sick man. He is so doped up it's a wonder he hasn't completely lost his mind.

I like Mohammed, but at times he can be annoying and a pest. He follows me all around the shelter nipping at my heels. I realize my surroundings are small and I have nowhere to hide—every time I look up, he is talking near my bunk or interrupting me. As long as I live here, I must put up with Mohammed and others like him.

monday, day 12

Another Monday. A fight breaks out. One man accuses another of cutting in line. It's not like they're serving eggs Benedict with white truffles on the side. The menu is cold cereal and coffee—no donuts—and these men are fighting over who is first. The shelter's policy is that fighting lands clients out on the streets. Neither of the men gets a chance to eat breakfast. I would have expected fighting to be an everyday occurrence, but this is the first fight I've seen so far. People have too much to lose in a shelter; getting thrown out means going without meals and a bed. Some homeless men are ex-cons, loose cannons, or street thugs, accustomed to violence. Most are not, though; they just want to be left alone. I applaud the shelter's policy of checking everyone for guns, knives, or anything that could be used as a weapon. I often wonder when someone will snap or go ballistic. The possibility is real and this is a frightening thought—it could happen at any moment. I worry about it.

Tomorrow twenty-four men from the shelter and I will begin a temporary job that will last a week. Every year a non-profit organization holds a mammoth book sale in a shopping mall. I'm told they will sell millions of books during the week-long sale. Our job will be to unload boxes and stock books into sections by subject. We will each be paid $5 an hour with a guarantee of eight hours per day.

We meet at Ivan's office to hash out the details. Ivan begins the meeting, "If I hear of anyone drinking on this job, you will be booted from the shelter," he says. Some men, including myself, have to be reminded about drinking on the job.

After the meeting with Ivan, I decide to fill out some more job applications. I continue to feel the pressure of not having a job that will allow me to save for an affordable apartment. Being jobless is trying for anyone. Everyone likes money in their pockets. Today I do more foot work. I catch more buses to more school districts. By now I'm tired, and my feet are hurting from walking all day in dress shoes instead of my comfortable three-year-old tennis shoes.

Back at the shelter everyone seems to be in a good mood. This evening a woman named Janet has brought the biggest and best Italian pizza I have ever tasted. On the side are fresh green salad, soft chocolate-chip cookies, natural sodas, and sweet, sliced oranges. People go back for seconds and thirds. Janet, only four foot, ten inches tall, is well known at the shelter for this big act of kindness. She buys this amount of food every year, paying for it out of her pocket. She doesn't act like a well-to-do person, but is open and affectionate with all who shake her hand. Her grandchildren help her during dinnertime. After the meal is served, she yells to one man to get a box out of her van. The box is filled with gloves, socks, toothbrushes, combs, hats, and shaving cream. I thank her and give her a kiss on the cheek for treating us with such rare kindness. Janet cares about homelessness. I will always remember her generosity and compassion. I go to bed thinking that her warmth and kindheartedness have given me some much-needed inspiration.

tuesday, day 13

It's 3:00 A.M., and I can't sleep. I feel alone and disoriented. Men are snoring all around me in the darkness. The man next to me is talking in his sleep, something about his ex-wife. Out in the front office the night manager is typing on a clackety manual typewriter.

I head to the restroom and find it looking like a mine field. Toilet paper is strewn all over the floor. Trash cans spill over. Near a toilet I notice three beer cans that someone has left behind. I avoid this stall because I might be accused of drinking. It's too early in the morning to be asked to leave. I return to my bed to sleep.

Three hours later, I catch a city bus for a forty-minute ride to begin unloading boxes of books. When we arrive at the mall, a woman greets us at three tractor trailers where the books are packed. I begin worrying about how my back will hold up. To my relief, we're told we will have several dollies for hauling books into the mall. This is good news. However, I am determined to work no matter how much pain I have. I cannot afford to blow an opportunity to make $200, which will be a good start toward my goal of saving for an apartment. The sooner the better, as each day gives me less time to save. Ivan is not really going to care if I meet my goal or not. I'm just another homeless guy passing through the system, and he's probably seen more failures than success stories.

After a few hours, I learn more about some of the men who are working with me today. During a brief break we stand around outside making small talk. An older man starts showing us his Texas prison ID card that he carries in his wallet as a reminder of serving fifteen years in prison for attempted murder and assault. He claims to have been free for two years and seems still to be adjusting to being free. One man jokes with him that he should throw his ID away unless he plans on visiting Texas soon.

Another man claims to have murdered a man in North Carolina and to have been convicted and served time. He tells us he murdered a man for raping a child while thirty adults stood by and watched. A judge gave him twenty years, but he says his sentence was later commuted by the governor of North Carolina after he served nine years.

The woman who hired us is busy inside the mall. Mohammed decides he will be foreman, giving everyone orders as the boxes come off of the trucks. We all become annoyed at his actions but go along with him as if he knows what he's talking about. Mohammed enjoys being the center of attention. Most of the men listen politely to him but do what they want. So far, no one has been seen drinking on the job, but in another trailer two men decide to smoke pot. The rest of us leave the area immediately, eighteen dollies going eighteen different directions.

Work today went well. The job doesn't require a great deal of brains. Before we check out for the day, we are split into two groups, a day crew and a night crew. I'm placed on the day shift.

wednesday, day 14

I awake with a clogged nose. The heater in the shelter isn't working, and I think I've caught a cold. I quickly shower, eat my breakfast, and leave for the book sale. The morning is spent stacking books under hundreds of tables inside the mall. This sale has every type of book imaginable, and every chance I get I try to browse without being seen by the woman who hired us. In her words, browsing will not be tolerated. She makes it clear: we have a job to do.

Before 5:00 P.M. we finish for the day. I catch a bus downtown and head back to the shelter. On the patio a bunch of guys are standing around a man who calls himself Tennessee, and he is carrying on about how various prescription drugs affect people. You would think him a trained pharmacist. He claims to buy and sell all types of medication drugs. Next, he tells everyone what street drugs he has taken. He's used cocaine and heroin, and he's a hard drinker. Tennessee has a broken arm from a bar fight. His speech is amusing at times, judging by how much people laugh at his stories.

I return to the barracks and go to my bunk. I realize my toiletry bag is missing. I'm outraged! Why me? I try to get along with people and mind my own business. In the shelter you hear of people having things stolen, and it does happen, but you never think it will happen to you. The day before, a man had an expensive leather jacket stolen from his bed. I try to keep my footlocker locked, but some things I don't keep there and, apparently, these are fair game. Toothpaste, dental floss, and soap are given out each morning for free—so why would someone steal mine? I start blaming myself for leaving the toiletry bag out. Maury says to check the front desk to see if it has been turned in. I begin laughing at the thought, but lo and behold, someone has found it and given it to a shelter manager. My attitude changes from outrage to embarrassment. Dumb me had left the bag in the restroom.

In the shelter one has to be concerned about catching germs. Some men do not wash their hands after using the restroom, and then they touch door handles, even serving utensils. The spread of germs is something to be concerned about, but there's one guy who takes it too far. When I enter the restroom, I see that the compulsive man is in front of a sink washing his hands. He washes repeatedly, at a steady pace, as though he's pushing toward the end of a marathon. No fingernail goes unscrubbed. The bar of soap grows noticeably smaller each time he uses it. He washes his hands for thirty minutes. His daily routine has become an obsession with taking precautions against catching a disease.

Then there's the other extreme. Some men simply cannot care less about personal hygiene. Others are unable to shower or shave. Tom, the old man in the wheelchair, has not changed his clothes, and no one has offered to help him, since I arrived here. Sleeping next to someone who hasn't showered in days is irritating, but in Tom's case, he is physically helpless. I have made up my mind to relocate to another bed as soon as I am able to talk to a shelter manager. Being around Tom wears me down.

It is late evening. Feeling like reading, I go to the library. I notice an old man reading a book in the corner. He's wearing mismatched shoes. I think this is all he can afford, but someone tells me the man refuses to wear matching shoes. No one knows why.

Living in the shelter has made me sharply aware of mental illness, a condition that is painful to observe. Sometimes mentally handicapped people appear to understand their world; other times they do not. Many mentally ill clients in the shelter can be spotted by their odd behavior. I've seen persons who isolate themselves, hear voices, alienate the people around them. Some are not on medication, and I notice they usually do not stick around the shelter for long.

thursday, day 15

Today is payday from the book sale. It gives me a chance to save toward my goal. Of the $200, 75 percent will go to Job Connection in a money order in my name to be held until I'm ready to move out on my own.

I flag down a bus and head to the Job Connection office to pick up the balance of my pay. I see Ivan hurrying from his office, holding a large brown paper bag to his side. He yells as he gets in his car that my pay will be given to me later at the shelter. I nod and say, "Okay." Suddenly it dawns on me that this guy might be skipping town with our money. That would be all I'd need, another scam artist taking what's mine.

I go back to the shelter to fill out more job applications and make follow-up phone calls. The applications are starting to become a custom, but the process is boring. Some are long and tedious, the activity is time-consuming. The long applications always require telling your entire life history. You would think the jobs paid six fig- ures. All I want is a job that will allow me to rent an apartment. I expect to live modestly. I rarely buy new clothes, and when I do I shop at a thrift store. One might call me frugal.

I'm also not into the bar scene; I have never liked the bar crowd. I'm a closet drunk, not your loud and sloppy drunk who wets his pants and vomits on your living room floor. I'm a quiet drunk, someone who keeps to himself and drowns in his misery and self- pity. I have never been an abusive drunk. But all drunks have one thing in common: a disease called alcoholism. The disease runs in my family. My mother died of liver disease from alcohol when I was eighteen. She was thirty-nine years old. My stepfather, a steel- worker who drank and used drugs, was physically and emotionally abusive toward my mother. I remember when I was about thirteen, he had been drinking and held a knife to her. And I remember on numerous occasions calling the police because he beat my mother so much. I wanted to kill him. He has since died of a heroin over- dose.

With alcohol comes such misery. Of my seven brothers, all have been heavy drinkers. Each one has been to prison or jail. Of my two sisters, one drank heavily for years but has since slowed down. The other was born with fetal alcohol syndrome. Somehow I have seen glimpses of a way out. I was able to become a Phoenix Suns ball boy, finish high school, join the navy, and graduate from col- lege, something that no one in my immediate family had ever accomplished.

With all of the odds against me, I often wonder how I was able to survive my family life in one of the poorest areas of south Phoenix. The navy helped me develop the character that I lacked growing up. Character came not only from discipline, but from a new struc- ture in life that I had never been exposed to. This experience made a man out of me at eighteen, though I still cannot understand why I chose the direction I did.

Later in the day I remember to call a few school districts for updates on the applications I have placed. My first call is to Baboquivari High School, located about fifty miles southwest of Tucson in Sells, Arizona.

Good news! The school district has received my paperwork. I'm given an assignment to teach high school social studies tomorrow. A woman on the phone instructs me to catch a coach bus at 6:45 A.M. at a pickup point. The school is on the Tohono O'odham Indian reservation, and the ride will take about an hour. I feel exhilarated and hopeful that an end to my homelessness may be in sight.

A short time later, Ivan arrives to pay us for our work at the book sale. A man named Billy Ray is first in line to be paid. His eyes are blazing like bonfires, and he appears to have been drinking or using drugs. Five men wait for him outside the shelter in a car with the motor running. Someone in line whispers that Billy Ray is a heavy drug user, and his money will be gone by tomorrow. Mohammed receives his money and leaves the shelter. I'm told he's back on drugs. My plan is simple and straightforward: I will get a money order and put my pay toward my savings.

Using the money for alcohol and drugs will only put me back into the skids. My success comes down to making the right choices. Each day is a challenge to stay clean and sober. Seeing people use alcohol and drugs around me on a daily basis makes it extremely difficult at times.

friday, day 16

The day I have been waiting for has finally arrived. Today I begin a
steady job. For almost three weeks I have pounded the pavement
to find steady work. Most men in the shelter are not in my position
to find work so fast. My college degree has its advantages. People
treat a man differently when he has above-average intelligence
and a diploma to prove it. When people in assistance agencies ask
me about the extent of my education, they then immediately ask,
"So why are you homeless?" I don't fit the stereotype of a homeless
person. My appearance is neat. I have never held a sign on a street
corner. I have never had to eat from a garbage Dumpster or sleep
in my vomit. I have never toted around a bedroll with all of my
belongings on my back, pushing a shopping cart.

Still just the mere fact of being homeless invites certain stereo-
types. It doesn't matter what color a homeless person is or how
much education he has, society seems unsympathetic. The homeless suffer most when applying for jobs and housing. Available jobs
never seem to pay enough to live on, and affordable housing is
scarce for those whose pay is at the low end of the wage scale.

After being out of work for weeks, it feels good to know I will once
again earn a paycheck. I've never taught on an Indian reservation
before, and I'm nervous. I take two city buses to the pickup point.
At 6:45 A.M., a charter bus pulls into the dirt parking lot behind an
ABCO grocery store. Teachers begin unloading their belongings
from their cars and head toward the bus. As I board, many of them
stare at me curiously, while others never see me and continue to
read their books and newspapers. I sit in an empty seat and start
reading my newspaper, feeling that these people act and look
ultra-conservative and unfriendly. I feel I don't belong. The shame
of being homeless overtakes me.

The ride toward Sells is scenic, with blooming plants abundant. The desert landscape has a quietness about it. I see an occasional coyote dead on the side of the highway and scavengers circling above. The teachers sit quietly or talk in whispers. Between reading the paper and looking out the window, I start to get restless as we get closer to the school.

A sign reads "Sells, Arizona, Estimated Pop. 2,035." The reservation looks deserted as the bus slows down. I'm surprised to see a small herd of cattle grazing unattended on the edge of the highway. This town has a sleepiness about it. Homes are probably left unlocked and everyone knows their neighbors. A teacher on the bus tells me the town has a very small police force, a post office, a grocery store, one hospital, two gas stations, one school district, and a tribal council and chairman as its government. The nearest bank is in Tucson.

On the right side of the road, a new school building sits off at a distance. The American flag waves in a steady wind as the bus turns into the school driveway, next to a sign that reads Baboquivari High School. Several teachers load into two vans for a ride to the primary school and intermediate school thirteen miles from town. My first impression of the high school is of tranquillity, especially compared to my last teaching job in Phoenix. The district is small, with a student enrollment of about 1,400.

High school students are offered an agriculture program, complete with cattle, sheep, and goats. In addition to taking the required courses in reading, writing, math, and the sciences, students are taught their native language and traditional culture. I'm told many students will not graduate from high school, and only a small percentage will go on to college. Absenteeism is extremely high, which explains why class sizes are between fifteen and twenty students daily at the high school. I come to sense a great deal of apathy, both from the students and the teachers. The students seem

51

not to value their education. A few students join gangs. Some show up for class and get by. Others just show up. A small number are quite bookish. One former student graduated from Stanford University.

I'm greeted in the school office by a large Tohono O'odham woman, who tells me where everything is located, hands me a room key, and sends me to a social studies class. At the teacher's desk the lesson plan awaits me with a message that most of my students will be on a field trip today. The students remaining in class will read from their textbooks. My job will be to answer any questions, take attendance, and manage the classroom.

The day goes smoothly. The students are well-behaved. In Phoenix, classes ranged from twenty-eight to thirty-two students. Today I have six students in each of my five classes.

The bus ride back to Tucson is more lively than in the morning. The teachers are laughing and joking. Going to work at five in the morning when most of America is still sleeping—not to mention riding a bus for two hours, five days a week—is not conducive to much socializing. Just the thought of this makes me wonder why these teachers do what they do. Is it because they enjoy teaching so much, or are these the only teaching jobs they can find? A few have been making this trip for years. I try reading on the way back to town but fall asleep instead. Before I know it, the bus is back in Tucson.

I catch a city bus back to the shelter, but stop first at Church's Fried Chicken for dinner. Later I'm glad I did because the dinner at the shelter is pinto beans, bread, coffee, and apples. I enjoy pinto beans, and they're good for you, but I wanted the best chicken on the planet.

When I walk in with my work clothes on, many men eyeball me

from head to toe. I'm wearing neatly pressed slacks, a dress shirt, a silk tie, and penny loafers. I get the impression they wonder who I am or what's wrong with me. After all, this is a homeless shelter, and men are not supposed to dress in this sort of attire.

I change into shorts, a T-shirt, and tennis shoes, and the gawking stops. I head to the patio to wind down and relax. No one asks me for a light or cigarette, which is surprising. Many men can't afford their own smokes, so they bum them from those who can afford them.

Today is a satisfying day—employment at last.

saturday, day 17

The weekend begins. I've decided to be the first in line to have my laundry done. Five minutes later, a Hispanic man joins me. He doesn't speak English. I explain the laundry procedure, but he doesn't understand what I'm saying. Finally, someone communicates with him in Spanish.

As I head back to my bunk, James is being informed that his time is up in the shelter. James's element is the streets, stealing and running hustles from parking garages to support his drug habit. His expression reveals a man uncertain about his future. Now where will he live?

My day begins with a trip to Reid Park, to the small zoo there that sits on seventeen acres, surrounded by two eighteen-hole golf courses, a duck pond, tennis courts, an indoor gymnasium, a band shell, a minor league baseball field, a rose garden, softball fields, lots of picnic spaces, and hundreds of huge shade trees. I enjoy my private time to relax, look at the animals, and walk around. I have had no urge to spend my time with men in the shelter. I'm thinking that for the most part we really don't have a lot in common. Time alone helps me think. After the zoo, I visit the library, but I don't stay long. I pass the time walking around downtown, thinking, and people-watching. Later, I return to the shelter for dinner.

As I enter the door, men are standing in line. Today's menu is a good one—turkey, fresh green salad, chili peppers, soft chocolate-chip cookies, and milk. After dinner, I read to pass time. I'm distracted as new clients are being interviewed by a social worker in the reading room. The question still fascinates me: How did these new clients become homeless? As I pretend to read, I eavesdrop on the interviews, which take less than ten minutes each, with questions ranging from personal history to current state of mind. I have decided to record these intakes so they can help me better understand why people fall down on their luck. Maybe I will gain insight from their experiences in life.

CLIENT INTAKE

A. White, 26 years old
B. High school dropout
C. Alcoholic—started drinking at age twenty-one
D. Drinking affects performance on job
E. Drinks any time of day
F. Becomes violent when he drinks
G. Family in Tombstone, Arizona, disowned him because of his drinking problem
H. Highly depressed

Social worker enrolls client in a social services program to treat alcoholism.

CLIENT INTAKE

A. White, 66 years old
B. High school graduate
C. Doesn't appear to have drug or alcohol problem
D. Homeless all of his adult life
E. Travels from state to state, living in homeless shelters
F. Has stayed in Primavera shelter on and off for eight years
G. Collects Social Security benefits
H. Seems normal

Social Worker recommends seven days in the shelter.

Someone might question whether I should listen to these interviews, but I'm curious about the reasons people become homeless. Each individual has a different story to tell. I thought homelessness was the guy pushing a shopping cart with a dog tied to it. I learn from each day of living in the shelter that anyone can hit rock bottom. I also see people who choose to be homeless. They enjoy living a meager life on the fringes of society. Personally I can't understand why some people prefer to be homeless. Sure, you can do as you please living outside of the norm, living in isolation with very little responsibility besides securing the basics such as food and shelter. In my opinion, this is no way to live. On the other hand, some people who end up homeless choose not to make homelessness a part of their lives any longer than necessary. In many instances they've fallen on hard times and are trying to bounce back and re-enter society.

sunday, day 18

I get out of bed, grab two boiled eggs and a donut, eat, and return to my warm bed. I pull the covers over my head to block out the glaring barracks lights. I want to fall back to sleep, but the loudspeaker's squawking and men moving about prevent me. Sleep is impossible with so much noise around.

I've made a decision today to join Prince Chapel. A client named Sal, the shelter's laundry attendant who once worked as a pharmacist and lost everything to a drug habit, lends me one of his sports coats and a dress shirt. As I get dressed, I feel apprehensive and sweat begins to dribble from my forehead. Joining a church means taking responsibility for attending on a regular basis. Christian fellowship brings new friends, but will I want to reveal that I am homeless? Many people have a negative attitude toward the homeless. Should I share my situation gradually? I want people to get to know me as a person, yet I want to be honest about living in a shelter and hold nothing back.

It's the first Sunday of the month, and this means Holy Communion. The service lasts for more than two hours. Today's sermon is about prayer in our daily lives, something I have been doing more of lately. The pastor explains that we cannot be true Christians if we only pray on Sundays. In his words, our lives as Christians are a daily matter of prayer and thankfulness to God. We must pray when things are both bad and good.

After the sermon, the pastor emphasizes that the church doors are open for membership. By now I'm really nervous and sweating profusely as I walk to the front of the altar. I feel like an unholy person requesting to enter into a family of Christians. All eyes in the sanctuary are on me, at least that's how it seems. After brief remarks from the pastor about joining the church, the members come up to me and another man and give us hugs and handshakes. I feel rejuvenated. At this moment, I don't feel like a homeless person. I'm engulfed with love and friendship.

I say good-bye and leave church on this emotional high. While I'm waiting for my bus, a late-model Mercedes-Benz with dark-tinted windows pulls up. A window rolls down.

"Would you like a ride home?" the woman passenger asks.

I hesitate. My shame about living in the shelter, which I dare not mention, floods my mind. There's no way I can allow these people to drive me home. One, it would make me uncomfortable with them. Two, how would it look, me getting out of a fancy car in front of the shelter?

"You can drop me off at the city bus station," I answer. I hop in the back seat for the five-minute drive. The two women introduce themselves. The driver happens to be the pastor's wife. She is very attractive, with cinnamon-colored skin and neat hair. Heavy jewelry glitters against her immaculate turquoise dress.

The passenger, also a member of the church, turns around and asks, "Where did you grow up?"

"Phoenix. I just moved to Tucson."

"Are you getting settled?" she asks in a friendly way.

"Yes."

"Where are you living?"

"I live in a boarding home." I say, hoping she will get the picture and not ask any more questions. Suddenly I find myself blurting out, "I live in a homeless shelter, out on Old Benson Highway."

Their reaction is puzzlement. I must not fit the stereotypical profile of a homeless person. But their reply to my situation demonstrates they are open-minded Christians. "It doesn't matter where you live," the pastor's wife says.

I feel good for being open. My address or the size of my bank account shouldn't matter. They drop me off at the bus station; I thank them and say good-bye.

The afternoon is winding down as I return to the shelter. My emotional high is slowly fading. Yet a part of me is still optimistic about the future. Sometimes one can find humor in the melancholy of shelter life. Sal, the laundry man, is shouting that someone has stolen all his socks from his personal laundry bag, which was on his bunk.

"I can't believe someone would commit such an act," he yells. "I pity the asshole who turns in the wrong pair of socks for washing." Everyone breaks out in laughter. Sal finds no humor in the situation.

In the restroom, the compulsive man is accused by another client of being gay because he spends so much time in front of a mirror close to the shower, brushing his teeth and washing. A verbal fight ensues, but no punches are thrown.

My euphoria from church disappears with all of the commotion around me. Shelter life can drain a man spiritually, emotionally, and mentally. However, humor can help one cope day to day. My objective is to get back on my feet and move on with my life. A person's surroundings clearly affect the emotional state, and my state of mind fluctuates each day I remain here. This day turns out to be

an emotional roller coaster, up and down. Will tomorrow be different, I wonder before going to sleep.

monday, day 19

A new week begins. I awake to a voice bellowing through a loud-speaker at the magic time of 5:00 A.M. I shower and dress and catch the two city buses to the shuttle bus for work on the reservation. Once again the shuttle bus is quiet as everyone keeps to themselves while we make the fifty-mile ride to school. I'm sleepy. The bus has reclining seats and rides like a Greyhound. A catnap is in order.

My assignment today is a seventh-grade social studies class. The lesson will cover mapping skills and how the British fought the Native Americans over land. The students and I read the text aloud together, and I answer a few questions. I ask a few students about the subject in hopes of engaging them in a dialogue to liven up the lesson. In college I minored in political science, so I enjoy teaching in this area. Having traveled to several countries with the navy doesn't hurt when comparing other political systems and linking my experiences with the lesson. My day goes without incident.

We leave the tiny town of Sells and arrive back in Tucson at 5:30 P.M. I decide to eat out again and have a craving for Mexican food. After grabbing a bite, I arrive at the shelter around 6:30 P.M. Manager Jon meets me at the door and asks for my name and bunk number. As I walk past the kitchen, the aroma sends chills through my body. It smells savory! This time I should not have eaten out because they're having lasagna tonight. Besides, eating out is getting expensive, not to mention my waistline is growing by the week.

After changing my clothes, I head to the patio. While I sit at a picnic table taking in the fresh air, two police officers drive up in front. We all want to know what's going on. The problem is a client who has been asked to leave for harassing Jon and for drinking inside the shelter. The officers handcuff the man and take him outside. One officer frisks the man and finds a small amount of pot. The man becomes abusive toward the officer. By now everyone is watching the incident and can't believe what's taking place. It seems right out of the TV show *Cops*. This guy's on his way to jail and everyone senses it.

The officers turn out to be good-natured and advise the cuffed man not to talk back. The man denies that the pot belongs to him and says it was planted in his pocket—a likely story. The patio erupts in laughter, and the cops chuckle as well. After a long pause, one cop begins lecturing the man about the law, adding some basic common sense, then lets him go his way with a warning that if he comes back on the premises he will be arrested for trespassing. The officers keep the pot. We can't believe they let this guy go. In some states a person is arrested for any amount of pot. In some countries the man would have paid even a bigger price. However, the officers must realize this man already has enough problems in his life. He doesn't need to go to jail for three lousy joints.

This excitement is the talk of the evening in the shelter. I'm feeling for the man because I know what he is going through. Addiction is powerful, for some an endless downward spiral that they never seem to escape.

tuesday, day 20

An old man across the barracks wets his pants and vomits all over the floor. The man is as sick as he was drunk the day before.

Time to take a shower. The compulsive man is hovering over a sink in front of the showers, washing his hands with soap up to his elbows. Everyone in the restroom seems to ignore him, going about their business, including me. Meanwhile, the paramedics are taking the sick man to the hospital.

I leave for work. Today I will teach high school students who are physically disabled; some have Down's syndrome and others have different mental disabilities. I fear the worst, anticipating that I will change diapers all day. But I find just the opposite. These kids are fun to work with, and they all have unique personalities. One student likes it when you sing nursery rhymes to him, like "Jack Sprat" or "Jack and Jill." This young man is twenty years old and has the mental ability of a five-year-old. His face lights up like a Christmas tree when someone sings to him. Another student with Down's syndrome enjoys listening to Michael Jackson music and gets upset if he doesn't get his way.

Much of the learning in this class focuses on basic life skills. The students are learning how to tie their shoes or how to tell time. They work on motor skills, such as putting a puzzle together or even taking daily walks. They learn basic cooking skills, such as frying an egg or baking cookies. The class has two full-time aides. The students have the bodies of adults and minds of children.

I sleep on the ride back to Tucson as the bus speeds down the narrow two-lane highway. Dotting both sides of the highway are grave markers of people who have died on this deadly route. Like most tribes, the Tohono O'odham have had problems with serious alcohol abuse, and this is evident by the markers of so many family members who have been killed in drunken-driving accidents. The lonely desert road is lit at night only with beams of light from speeding cars.

The bus arrives in Tucson, and I catch two city buses back to the shelter, where I notice fifteen new clients getting off the shelter bus. Most of the men look as if they have spent days on the street. One guy is wearing old shoes with little left of the soles. A clamorous flop echoes as he crosses into the reading room for his intake interview. His hair is as tangled and dust-filled as tumbleweeds. Another man's face is dirty from going days without a shower. Another carries several bags, and a stench follows him through the room. Each man seems tired, hungry, and relieved to know that tonight he will be able to shower, eat a hot meal, and sleep in a clean bed.

I remember the first night I walked into the shelter from the cab, empty and angry at myself for allowing this to happen. I've made some bad choices. Here, I have a chance to clean up and get back on my feet. Today I have a job. Today I have a place to live.

I've been able to acquire a few good clothes, courtesy of the shelter, which has a shed full of donated clothes. I find out later that a new tweed jacket I picked out had been donated by an elderly woman after her husband died. She gave his entire wardrobe to the shelter. I wear on my back a dead man's jacket, a true testament to my homelessness. Donations are what keep shelters afloat. Private and civic donations include money, bikes, furniture, food, sporting goods equipment, cooking equipment, blankets, shoes, and clothes. Some people donate things without much thought, such as treadmills, coffee tables, yogurt makers, egg poachers, and camper shells. One woman even donated a trampoline. However, some things do benefit the homeless. In the shelter if you need clothes, you simply place your name on a list for what is called a "clothing run," a free shopping spree in a shed filled with ties, shoes, boots, gloves, underwear, socks, pants, jackets, shirts, belts, hats, sunglasses, and the like. Because of this service, I can be presentable for teaching.

Men line up as dinner is approaching. Clients with disabilities are first in line. Tonight we have Tom and another man in their wheelchairs. The other men and I wait patiently to be served. Dinner consists of a rice casserole, coleslaw, chicken salad, orange juice, and fresh rolls.

While in line, I overhear a young Hispanic man telling an older white man that he has been able to abstain from having sex. The young man says it's been two years since he had sex with a female. The older man claims he's abstained for years but gives no exact time frame. For me, it's been more than six months since I saw my girlfriend in Phoenix before coming to Tucson. I'm afraid now of catching AIDS. In my navy days, I think I slept with a woman in every country I visited, but my sleeping-around days ended more than 15 years ago. AIDS awareness has made me stop my promiscuity to reduce my risk of contracting that disease.

While I am in the reading room, Jon catches three other managers smoking pot in the back of the shelter, an area that is off-limits to clients. We hear later that each manager is written up and given a stern warning that if such an infraction happens again he will be fired. The rule of thumb is, if you're staff, you basically have the run of the place. Managers take advantage of this privilege all of the time. Once a donation of new jackets came in, and the managers got first choice. They can raid the refrigerator at any hour, yet clients cannot. They can leave the shelter at anytime, clients cannot. Clients caught smoking pot are thrown out while managers keep their jobs. Managers can park their cars around the shelter, while clients owning vehicles must park them in a nearby shopping mall parking lot and run the risk of something happening to the cars.

But again, who am I?

wednesday, day 21

Today's teaching assignment is the same as yesterday's. I work with a student named Russell—the Michael Jackson enthusiast—who has Down's syndrome. He can listen to his music all day if you let him. He even tries Michael's dance moves. He is affectionate and laughs constantly despite his disability. Russell seems not to have a worry about the little things in life. He also seems to be at peace with himself as well as with the people around him. Although his learning is extremely limited, he has a big heart. My day is a pleasant one. Russell helps me realize that even if someone has a disability or hardship, he can still be in good spirits. Russell doesn't express this thought verbally, but his eyes and warm smile express what life is all about. Everyone has problems, but how we deal with them is what really matters.

Upon arriving back at the shelter, I'm greeted by several new clients waiting in a line near the reading room to meet with a social worker. Tonight's dinner has been prepared by a local church and consists of macaroni/tuna without any flavor, stale bread with hard crust, tiny cups of peaches, and coffee that has perked too long. After dinner, I decide to eavesdrop on tonight's intake interviews.

CLIENT INTAKE
A. White, 42 years old
B. Talks fast
C. Air Force veteran
D. Homeless since 1986
E. Has no income
F. Admits he is a paranoid schizophrenic

Social worker places the client in a social service program to assist those with mental illnesses.

A. White, 44 years old
B. Native of Texas
C. Recently involved in a motorcycle accident and wears a beard to cover facial scars
D. Non-drug user
E. Moderate drinker
F. Homeless two days
G. Wants to find work

Social worker enrolls the client in the Job Connection program for four to eight weeks.

CLIENT INTAKE
A. White, 35 years old
B. Extremely long hair
C. Non-vet
D. Needs money to return to Michigan because his mother is dying of cancer
E. Distraught
F. Homeless two weeks
G. Suffers from seizures, has taken medications since 1961

Social worker recommends a two-week stay in the shelter for the client, who must find day labor jobs that pay daily.

CLIENT INTAKE
A. White, 39 years old
B. Holds a college degree in psychology from the University of Arizona
C. Non-veteran
D. On anti-depressive medication
E. Homeless one month

F. Seeks employment in social work field

G. Seems apprehensive

Social worker recommends Job Connection program for four to eight weeks.

Today has again been a learning experience as I hear new guys tell their life stories. In them I see myself, just wanting someone to stop and listen to my story.

thursday, day 22

I arrive at work at 8:20 A.M. with the same assignment as yesterday. The day goes fine until a student, the one who likes nursery rhymes, flies out of control. He's swinging at everything in his path. I go to grab him and am struck by a flying fist in the face. This guy is strong. The punch pushes me back two steps. An aide steps in and begins singing, "Twinkle, twinkle, little star," and the student immediately calms down as though he is hypnotized. I watch in disbelief as I shake off his punch. The incident brings back memories of my previous run-in with a special education student when I injured my back. The rest of the day comes and goes, and I can say I made it through another school day.

Later, back at the shelter, an altercation breaks out in the kitchen at dinner. One of the servers, a client, refuses to give another client in line an extra slice of cornbread. Typically, second servings are only handed out after everyone has eaten. I later find out the real reason for this argument: the client has accused the server of making sexual advances toward him, which he had refused earlier. The argument between the two men becomes loud, and except for their fighting, there is dead silence in the small dining hall. The two begin punching each other on the floor, and both men are thrown out of the shelter for fighting. This whole episode is childish, two grown adults fighting over sex and a slice of cornbread.

Some people at the shelter add pleasantness to the place. Blondie, the barber, is a diminutive woman who cuts hair for a living in an upscale beauty shop. Once a week she volunteers her comb and scissors to cut the hair of the homeless. She even has time to give me a few pointers. Blondie loves what she is doing. She mentions how clients tell her that they landed a job after a new haircut. Blondie puts in twelve- to fifteen-hour days, yet somehow finds time to offer free haircuts two hours a week at the shelter.

While certain people such as Blondie become familiar, others stand out in that they make you uneasy each time you see them. For the past three weeks I have noticed a Hispanic man in his fifties or sixties who sprays Lysol in his mouth every night to get a buzz. He stuffs toilet paper between his legs and buttocks before he goes to bed. He's worn the same shirt and pants even though free clothes are handed out every night. His hair resembles Albert Einstein's. He catches the shelter bus into town every morning and spends his time at the public library, not reading but talking out loud; people pass by and ignore his comments as though he's not there. Like many clients, he just disappears one day.

friday, day 23

Working on the reservation has meant that I eat my breakfast and lunch on campus. The prices are reasonable. Breakfast is $0.75 and lunch is $1.50.

Today's assignment is at the high school. The lesson for the day is in art. Many O'odham students appreciate art, which is evident from the great Native American work I see in the classroom—weaving, red pottery, and works on canvas. Many of the students' paintings reflect the hardships of their lives—abuse, suicide, anger, pain—as well as details of their desert landscape. Giant murals adorn the campus. The tribe is known for producing artists. Many students go on to study at the well-known Native American Art Institute in New Mexico.

After work I return to the shelter. The evening is winding down, and I join others on the patio. A client who has been in the shelter for a month begins smoking pot just as the sun is setting. He is unaware that a manager is standing a few feet away as he takes a few drags from his weed. Five minutes later, he is asked to pack his bags and leave immediately.

More patio activity: Three men begin debating, "Who was the first to sin?" One says, "It was Eve." Another says, "Adam." The third man also says, "Adam." A few minutes later, several other men join in on this religious topic. Tempers begin to flare over the question. I was once told never to debate religion, politics, or sex with those who do not share your views. It will likely end up at an impasse.

Inside the shelter men are sitting around on their bunks. Some talk to each other while a few stay to themselves. A manager named Carlos walks around sprinkling foot powder in clients' shoes if they give off any bad odor. On this day, 90 percent of the shoes, including my own, receive fresh powder.

In this place I've learned to get to know as few people as possible. I place no trust in the majority of the people here. Even though I've met some guys I can talk with, I will only go so far. Let's just say I wouldn't hand over my paycheck to someone to hold for me and expect it to be available when I wanted it. Some men don't care to be trusted, and others don't care if you care. There's an attitude of what's mine is mine, and the minute you let your guard down, yours will be mine.

Mohammed tells me, "This place is exactly like prison, with one exception: You can leave any time you want."

He may be right. I've never been incarcerated, but I once toured a prison with a sociology class in college. I remember similarities. All African American inmates hung together, as did whites and Hispanics. Men do the same in the shelter. In prison, guards watch your every move, drill the rules into you, and punish you when you disobey. You're told how to live from day to day whether you like it or not. In prison, cigarettes can buy you anything, I'm told. In the shelter, that's half-true. I've yet to see anyone shanked over a carton of cigarettes or raped for a pack. But I have seen men trade packs for shoes, belts, hats, bus tickets, drugs, prescription medications, food stamps, cassette players, beer, and food. I remember one guy ran out of smokes one night, and some guy sold him a pack for $5. Several men roll their own cigarettes and sell them for a quarter.

Each day I'm here brings new observations, new challenges, and I can only take them one day at a time.

saturday, day 24

Gus, the shelter bus driver, is cursing loudly in front of the office window. Someone has broken into the bus overnight. Apparently, the only items taken were emergency road flares. Gus becomes so irate that his face turns chili pepper red. He weighs more than three hundred pounds, wears farmer overalls, and arrives with a briefcase every morning. At least seventy years old, he wears thick bifocals. He can curse with the best, though he is good-natured and loves to sit and tell shelter stories. The old bus is his life. Fond of big vehicles, Gus drives a dump truck for his personal use. One manager tells me Gus lives alone and is a recovering alcoholic. It doesn't matter what was stolen from the bus—someone has violated him. He's pissed!

Gus's rage this morning makes me want to walk downtown. There is nothing like a mad driver behind the wheel. The walk is less than two miles. On the way, I run into Lamar, the recovering drug addict and alcoholic who now lives in transitional housing managed by Primavera. This program offers affordable housing for the poor. You can come and go as you wish, and you provide your own food. Lamar pays only $100 per month and shares a room with a roommate. We exchange greetings and swap shelter gossip. Lamar looks great! He looks and acts like a sober and clean person. His sobriety has landed him a job and a home.

The hour is early, and Lamar talks me into donating plasma as a way to make a quick $25. By bringing me in as a first-time donor, he will receive a $5 bonus for the referral. I agree to give it a try. I really need some extra cash, and donating plasma is a way to earn, plus maybe my plasma will save a life. Regular plasma donors regard it as having a part-time job. Lamar says he knows one man who does it to pay his $100-a-month rent. It is possible, because a person can donate twice a week and receive $15, $20, $25, and $30 in succession.

Plasma centers have specials every month allowing donors to earn bonus cash. It is not uncommon to earn $165 per month. My intention is to donate so that I'm able to make it between the two-week pay periods. I've donated plasma in the past, and it's a relatively simple process. A physician gives you a complete physical to check for AIDS, hepatitis, drugs, or alcohol.

The procedure is safe. Needles and plasma bags are always new. Phlebotomists use plastic gloves every time they stick you with a needle. New phlebotomists can't stick you until they've completed months of training. The blood is separated from the plasma and returned to your body. On rare occasions a donor is injured or faints.

As I begin filling out the new donor application, a woman asks me for my picture ID. I hand her my driver's license. She pronounces that I cannot donate because I live in a homeless shelter. Why? Homeless people move around too much, and the homeless run a greater risk of catching diseases, she tells me. I'm upset after being turned down, but I accept it and go on my way.

On my way out, I recognize four familiar faces from the shelter, including the old man who went through the windshield. I try to make eye contact with him, but he acts as if he has never seen me before in his life. I understand that he doesn't want to blow his chances of donating. The other three men hold their heads down, praying I won't blurt out that I know them from the shelter. Lamar is handed bad news as well. His test results came back from the lab indicating he has hepatitis B, and he can no longer donate plasma anywhere in the country.

Next I stop over at the University of Arizona's main library for research and to read a bit. While I'm there I strike up a conversation with a graduate student working the information booth who describes his recent homeless experience after I ask him where I might find information about homelessness.

He gives an account of his homelessness four months ago, how he lost his home, a girlfriend, and his job due to an injury he suffered, which he chooses not to disclose. The man tells me he became a recluse and didn't believe in turning to social agencies or homeless shelters for help. He says he was able to survive by living in a friend's backyard, with occasional stops at his parents' home. Finally, he decided life was worth living, and he turned his life around and returned to school. He will graduate with a master's degree in the spring.

His will not to quit is inspiring. I walk away feeling uplifted. What a day! From starting out with an angry bus driver and meeting a friend who discovers he has hepatitis, it ends with being inspired by a former homeless man who beat the odds.

sunday, day 25

I'm feeling good today. After breakfast I return to my bed for a quick catnap before morning cleanup begins. Later Carlos, the shelter manager, asks me to help him clean the shower stalls. Not the normal quick cleanup, this job requires scrubbing with strong chemicals to get rid of germs that tend to build up. The toxic chemicals clear out the shelter. I can't stand it myself and head to the fresh air outside.

After the smell of chemicals has dissipated, I return to my bunk and take another nap. The rest of the day I spend reading and preparing for the week ahead. I iron my work clothes. Maury, the salesman, is telling jokes on the patio. Some are good, some corny, all clean. Sometimes he gets on a roll and attracts an audience.

Tonight it is quiet inside the shelter. Just as I notice this, a police helicopter begins to search a field nearby and circles with its light beams for over an hour. We watch from the dining room window to see what's going on. Suddenly the helicopter disappears into the dark night.

It's getting late. I read more of *Soul On Ice*, Eldridge Cleaver's book about prison life in the 1960s. I take a shower before going to bed. The compulsive man is cleaning himself at his usual spot. It's 10:30 P.M. when I call it a day and go to bed.

monday, day 26

Monday again. My assignment today is a high school home eco-
nomics class. I take this opportunity to share with the students how
I learned to cook while in the navy. I was eighteen and had flown
to the Philippines to join my shipmates aboard the aircraft carrier
USS Kitty Hawk, a floating city on water, with a crew of five thousand men. The ship had eighty jets on the flight deck and a brig
run by the U.S. Marines. Three days in the brig meant three days
of bread and water. I was told to report to the general kitchen, or
mess as they called it, to begin my navy career as a mess management specialist—or cook. Some fat guy asked me if I knew anything about cooking. I replied that I didn't. He handed me a metal
spatula and told me to start grilling four thousand pork chops on a
hot griddle. I became so good at grilling I soon graduated to making instant mashed potatoes to feed the entire crew. The first time I
baked homemade pies was a disaster. I mixed the dough with hot
water and the crust was harder than steel. A few years later I was
promoted and cooked for admirals and officers aboard smaller
ships. The students seem to enjoy these stories.

It's been another good day teaching. Back at the shelter, I'm
unable to listen in on intakes because the interviews are switched
to an area that is off-limits.

Every Monday a team of registered nurses and a doctor give free
medical checkups and referrals. I have my blood pressure checked
because I have been tired lately. When I was a child I was diag-
nosed as having the sickle-cell anemia trait. My blood pressure is
found to be okay—138/82—yet I'm advised to lay off smoking. I
currently smoke about a pack a day. I started smoking at twenty-
six when I entered college. Old habits are hard to kick. Like all

addictions, smoking controls you until you find the will to want to change.

Tonight I watch as the compulsive man begins his nightly ritual. He starts by washing the hot and cold knobs near the face bowl with a toothbrush. He then places paper towels all around the counter. Next, he places soap, dental floss, toothbrush, and toothpaste on the paper. He flosses his teeth for what seems like hours, but I can't bear to stick around.

It is another quiet night in the shelter. The barracks area is pitch dark as the men sleep. The only noise in the building is the night manager typing up his reports. In addition to the Cleaver book, I'm still reading *The Firm* by John Grisham. I have never been one to read a book in a day like some people. I'm enjoying this page turner, though, with its great suspense.

tuesday, day 27

The workday has arrived again. Today's assignment is junior high math and social studies. It doesn't take long to establish a reputation as a good or bad sub. Teachers and students talk. Most students enjoy subs who are nice and give as little work as possible in the absence of their regular teacher. Teachers pray that they will return to a normal class and find you've followed their lesson plans. It's a balancing act. I try to keep both sides happy. Sometimes this works and sometimes it doesn't.

Since I've been here, I've had fewer behavior problems from the students than I had in some inner-city schools where I averaged five office referrals a week for discipline-related offenses.

Another workday under my belt. The ride back into town is relaxing and I enjoy the green desert scenery and majestic mountains. A hawk flies above the bus as we travel through the heat of the afternoon.

Back at the shelter, dinner is about to be served; it's a good one— beef Stroganoff with a savory sauce, fresh tossed green salad, soft raisin cookies, and ice-cold fruit punch. While standing in line for dinner, I strike up a conversation, as I normally do. A client in his forties talks about riding freight trains for the past twelve years. He loves it despite its danger. Recently, he rode in by train from Boston.

"One time I almost killed myself jumping off a train in Texas," he says. "I landed wrong when I jumped off a moving train, and I ended up in the hospital for two months with a broken leg and broken arm."

After dinner, I realize tonight's intakes are being held in the reading room—my chance for more eavesdropping. The people in the room have no idea what I'm really doing as I pretend to read and take notes. However, before listening in on the interviews tonight, I discuss my motivation with Ashley, the social work intern. She has no problem with it. In fact, she thinks it's a great idea. Tonight, I record four more client intakes.

CLIENT INTAKE
A. Native American, 64 years old
B. Homeless for one month
C. Army veteran
D. On Social Security
E. Reports no drug or alcohol problem
F. Just passing through town from New Mexico

Social worker recommends two-week stay in the shelter.

CLIENT INTAKE
A. African American, 23 years old
B. Recovering alcoholic
C. Treated in three rehab centers for alcoholism
D. Wants to enter rehab again
E. Homeless for one month
F. Has lived in Tucson for one year
G. Suffers heart block, which causes low heart rate; takes large dosages of aspirin

Social worker recommends client go into social services program for alcoholism treatment.

CLIENT INTAKE
A. White, 54 years old
B. Alcoholic for ten years
C. Says he goes to jail every time he drinks

D. Has never sought treatment
E. Homeless ten months
F. Suffers from sleep disorder

Social worker enrolls client in social services program to treat alcoholism.

CLIENT INTAKE
A. White, 31 years old
B. Unemployed
C. Says dead-end job forced him to become homeless
D. States he needs dental work
E. Appears to have no physical or mental disabilities

Social worker recommends Job Connection program and state-run health plan.

I gather up my notes and reflect on the men's stories. Tired and sleepy, I climb into bed and call it a day.

wednesday, day 28

The bus ride each morning is taking its toll on me, so today I'm relieved not to work on the reservation. I'm scheduled to attend a substitute teachers' orientation with Tucson Unified School District (TUSD), which has more than one hundred schools scattered around the Tucson area. This orientation is mandatory before any assignments are given out.

I eat breakfast at the shelter. Several men begin yelling that their eggs are not hard-boiled but raw. I check mine, and they are also raw. A few other men find hard-boiled eggs instead of raw ones. For a minute, I think people will start throwing their eggs at the cook, but instead, we all just shrug off the mishap and continue eating our breakfast.

I catch a city bus for the three-hour orientation. The facilitators cover everything from A to Z about district policy. I anticipated the orientation would be a waste of time and boring, but it turns out to be informative.

Most school districts hand you a booklet to read about their policies and throw you to the wolves. Because of its size, this district tries to head off substitute teachers' problems. The pay is $48 per day. On the reservation they pay $55 per day. The pros and cons balance each other out. If I sub on the reservation, I earn more and my day ends at 5:00 P.M. If I sub in town, I earn less and my day ends at 3:00 P.M.

On the bus ride back from the orientation, I recognize a client from the shelter who is drunk. Every night he has been drunk, yet he goes unnoticed by the managers. He's the kind of drunk who will pick a fight if you look at him the wrong way. I suppose he's a good guy when he is not drinking. On the bus he is rude and disrespectful to anyone who crosses his path. I reflect how powerful booze really can be. Some of us cannot handle it, and this man is a testimonial.

Back in the shelter, a client is enraged after being told the restroom and shower are closed for late-morning cleaning. The man just loses it. He lowers his pants in front of the office window and eliminates his waste right on the floor. The manager on duty is Jon, the one no one likes. This altercation started with Jon's nasty tone when he told the guy the restroom and shower were closed. This man really had to use the restroom badly. Surely Jon saw this but wanted to show the guy that he was in charge and could make him wait. The man is asked to leave the shelter, and Jon is stuck with cleaning up the mess.

Since I have been here I have seen men thrown out of the shelter for various rules violations, such as fighting, drinking, using drugs, breaking curfew, failing to save in the Job Connection program, eating or smoking in the barracks, refusing to shower, being a pain in the neck. One guy was even thrown out for kicking Rambo. The cat has never been the same since.

Yet I often think about how good we have it. The rewards are not the greatest, but when I compare what we have to life on the streets, the shelter offers a great deal. What we wouldn't have outside the shelter includes housing, clothing, three meals a day, medical attention, employment resources, counseling, transportation, cable TV—and an opportunity to gain back our self-esteem. It puzzles me when guys fail to see this and choose to live on the streets or move from shelter to shelter. At the same time, I know I can be concerned only about me. My options are the same as theirs. A clear mind has helped me to stay on course. Each day is a challenge to continue this journey, and some days are better than others. Another day. I must get ready for tomorrow.

thursday, day 29

I return to the reservation. My assignment is to teach high school world history, U.S. history, and Arizona government—subjects that are of special interest to me. I enjoy political science, especially the U.S. presidency and international politics. In college, I was an active member in the Model United Nations Club. Students are dismissed early today, so the bus arrives back into town at 3:30 P.M., ahead of the usual time. My lower back is aching, and I'm tired. Back at the shelter, nap time.

I awake just in time for dinner, which is sponsored tonight by a youth organization. Having teenagers serve dinner to us is a great idea. Not only can they feel a sense of pride and accomplishment, but they also get a feel firsthand for what homelessness is all about. They see that homeless people are human beings. Above all, it is an education that they will never receive in the classroom. I hope they will educate friends and family members about their experience.

I find that I write just about anywhere in the shelter—the dining room, patio, barracks, restroom, and the reading room. After dinner I get out my note pad and begin recording notes on tonight's intakes.

CLIENT INTAKE
A. White, 77 years old
B. World War II veteran
C. Suffers from post-traumatic stress disorder
D. Wife ran off with another man
E. Recovering alcoholic
F. Homeless three years
G. Stayed in shelter three years ago

Social worker refers client to social services for several issues.

CLIENT INTAKE

A. African American, 45 years old
B. Recovering alcoholic
C. Substance-abuse history
D. Collects Social Security benefits
E. Homeless for ten years
F. Has had five open-heart surgeries; wears a pacemaker.

Social worker recommends that the client enroll in drug- and alcohol-abuse treatment program.

It's 10:00 P.M. I play a game of chess with David in the dining room before going to bed. The TV is off. The lights are off in the barracks. A client comes in and starts mumbling that he wants to watch the *Twilight Zone*. Someone yells out, "Just sit down and watch a few men in the shelter." Laughter erupts, but this man is serious about his request. After realizing the TV is not going to be turned on, he storms out of the dining room into the dark barracks, pissed off. Those of us left in the room laugh hard at what has just taken place.

friday, day 30

T.G.I.F. I hurry to catch the bus to work. My assignment today is high school English. I will receive my first paycheck after work. My savings so far total $400 toward my goal of $1,000. I have four more weeks in the program.

The school day is typical of any other. The lesson plan calls for me to talk about the different parts of a persuasive paper, and I help students with writing speeches. For most people, giving a speech can be a frightening experience, and the students are uncomfortable with the assignment. They seem at ease writing a speech but become terrified at delivering the short five-minute talk in front of the class.

After work, I go to church to see about joining the choir. A member goes out of her way to persuade me to join. Ever since I was a child, gospel music has appealed to me. Gospel music is uplifting, and I can use some uplifting right now. I feel alone. Two hours of singing brightens up my evening.

On my way back to the shelter, I get a wild hair and start thinking about moving into an apartment tonight. But as I think more about moving out of the shelter, it makes less sense to me. Sure, I have enough money to pay rent, but not enough for other things I will need such as food, utilities, spending money, and the like. I've gone this far, what's four more weeks? Often quick decisions are later regretted. Having $1,000 versus $400 just makes better practical sense. I'll stay with my plan.

A heavy rain is falling, and the shelter is overflowing with new clients who want to get out of the wet night. The place is almost filled to capacity. I'm resting on my bunk when a man tries to sell me his food stamps. For $50, I would get a value of $112. I decline the man's offer. This guy is a known heroin addict and is trying to get a fix. Plus I don't need any more headaches than I already have.

Twenty minutes later, a drug addict wants to sell me his Walkman that doesn't work for $10. When I say no, he gets a confused look on his face as if surprised that I refuse to buy a broken cassette player. This guy will not give up. He tries to sell the Walkman to several other men, but all turn him down. I'm thinking to myself, this guy needs some help, and I remember the Rev. Jesse Jackson's phrase, "Up with hope, down with dope."

Today turned out to be a bizarre mix of up and down, but somehow I kept my sanity. By the grace of God I survived another day here.

saturday, day 31

This morning I learn that on the third Saturday of every month a church serves a hot breakfast to the homeless at Santa Rita Park, a haven for homeless street people, the true hard-core of the homeless.

I find the park crowded with families and men and women, hefting backpacks, pushing shopping carts. The client who took a dump in front of the office window is in line. He appears to be living on the streets, judging by the way his dirty clothes look. He looks like he's lost weight from not eating. He looks awful, all trembling and green about the gills, like a sick frog with shell shock.

Over a hundred people are attracted to the hot breakfast of scrambled eggs, sausage, flour tortillas, hot coffee, and cold orange juice. The group sponsoring this event is the Northwest Community Friends Church of Tucson. Volunteers like these provide a valuable service to the homeless population, many of whom sleep under bridges and in parks, eating many meals from Dumpsters. These are the homeless no one wishes to encounter, the homeless who have urinated on themselves and smell of it, the homeless who are seen passed out on benches, in doorways. They are the ones who haven't shaved or bathed in days. I needed this experience to get a feel for what the hard-core homeless go through day to day. Their faces tell the story of survival and of the seriousness and depth of homelessness in our society.

After eating and watching, I catch a bus to see a matinee of *Philadelphia*, starring Tom Hanks and Denzel Washington. Later I catch another bus to go to LensCrafters to have my eyes examined. Next, I catch one more bus downtown and just walk around and take in the nice weather.

At last, I return to the shelter. I notice a new client, an African American in a wheelchair. As I'm sitting on my bed, he wheels up and introduces himself to me. His name is Howard. He asks me if I would cut his hair. I thought my hair-cutting days were over. I agree to cut his hair for free, but he insists that I take $2. We begin talking while I'm cutting his hair and I notice how clear-headed this guy seems. He spits out words with ease and doesn't fit the typical homeless stereotype. When I finish cutting his hair I have learned some interesting things about him.

Born in Canada, Howard attended college at the University of Quebec and Penn State. He studied architectural landscape, has a bachelor's degree, and has completed graduate work. He speaks Spanish, French, Italian, Arabic, Japanese, Greek, German, Latin, Korean, Russian, and Portuguese. He had a near-fatal accident while working in construction. He fell 150 feet and broke his neck. He's paralyzed from his waist down. Hospitalized over six months, he had medical bills of more than $400,000. He is suing his company for negligence, but his case has been in the courts for two years. Howard was mugged recently by three men who robbed him and stabbed him in the shoulder. A long scar confirms this part of the story.

Howard's story gets worse. His house, which was under construction, burned down. Despite all that has happened to him, Howard doesn't seem to have thrown in the towel.

"I'm still alive," he says. "I can only thank the man upstairs."

sunday, day 32

I awake and realize my black dress slacks are missing. Our choir
will sing this morning at church, and we are required to wear
black. Last night, I hung the pants over my bunk rail, I thought. In
an hour and a half, I must be at church. I look high and low for my
pants. I even offer a reward for their safe return. A half-hour later I
locate the pants hanging on a rack inside the shelter clothing closet. They are tagged with a sticker listing the length and waist size,
ready to be donated to any client at the shelter. My only guess is
that the pants fell off my bed. I hurry to dress for church and arrive
on time. Singing this morning is inspiring and uplifting.

The sermon today discusses the "Power of Christian Peace." Our
pastor maintains that a Christian person is more prepared to deal
with adversity. People without Christ have little peace and are
uncertain or confused about life, the pastor says.

After service, I'm invited by an older couple from the choir for
Sunday dinner at their home. We feast on Southern fried chicken,
mustard greens, mashed potatoes with gravy, and sweet corn
bread. The meal is absolutely delicious. I'm stuffing myself until
each button on my shirt feels like it will pop off. I have to loosen
my belt so I can breathe.

I arrive back at the shelter at 6:00 P.M., finding it quiet with everyone in a relaxed mood. Several men are watching TV, others are
filling out job applications in the reading room. Two men play a
game of chess. I like playing chess because it's a lot like life—you
must think on your feet and make good decisions. I've never mas-
tered the game.

In homelessness, my days, too, are like playing chess. The choices

I make dictate how well I'll do in the end. My homelessness is "check" and I have to make the right decisions to avoid being placed into "checkmate." With booze in my life, I remain in a stalemate on the brink of defeat. Without booze, I have a much greater chance of winning.

monday, day 33

Soon after the lights come on, a client is running through the shelter, seething. He'd taken a shower, set his watch down in the restroom, and forgotten when he toweled off to pick it up. Hours later he remembered where he had left it, but, as one might expect, the watch was not there. The client is furious and pained, as if someone has died. He shrieks about the watch being a gift from his grandmother, a diver's watch with a bunch of gizmos on it. He offers a reward for the watch's return, and in the back of my mind I have this feeling the watch will turn up. Sure enough, a man comes forward claiming to have found the watch in the restroom. The owner offers only a handshake as the reward. The man who turned in the watch appears disappointed, seeming to have wanted more than a handshake. Everyone else agrees.

Keeping time is what most homeless people do best—with or without a watch. Time to work. Time to find food. Time to find shelter. Time to move on. Time to panhandle. Time to drink away the pain. Time to stay warm. Time to ask for help. The homeless know what time it is. It's time to survive.

You might think that in a homeless shelter no one would have anything worth stealing. Yet many guys have Walkmans, cartons of cigarettes, clothes, shoes, jewelry. One guy even collects cigarette lighters. In the real world, these items are mostly minor conveniences. In the shelter, they're big-ticket items. Most clients come into the shelter with little or nothing. The belongings you do have, some you cherish and others you take for granted. For each person, what matters is different. The only items I don't lock up are my shoes and a few books I have placed over my bunk. You can't trust anyone. If a guy will steal your dirty socks, then anything is possible.

I leave for work. Today's assignment is high school physical education. The lesson plan calls for basketball in the main gymnasium. I take attendance and put out six basketballs; the students play three-on-three games for the class period. My job is to make sure no one kills anyone else in the process. After work, I return to the shelter for an afternoon nap.

The volunteers for tonight's dinner are Sally and Company, a group of women who have been cooking for the shelter for more than six years. This is the healthiest meal I have eaten since I've been here. The menu includes a cold tuna casserole garnished with ripe tomatoes; fruit salad topped with raspberry yogurt and mint leaves; tossed green salad with romaine lettuce; soft, fat-free, chocolate-chip cookies; whole wheat bread without butter; and pink lemonade.

People gather on the patio to talk after dinner. Maury, the salesman, is poking fun at the compulsive man. "The freak is in the shower soaping himself down, then looks down and sees a cavity in place of his privates," he says. After the laughter subsides, someone raises the question, "Is the compulsive gay or just weird?" I think the guy is just plain weird.

Several new faces come in tonight, and I feel like listening in on intakes.

CLIENT INTAKE
A. African American, 31 years old
B. College graduate
C. Addicted to crack cocaine
D. Homeless six months
E. Awaiting settlement from medical malpractice suit from father's death
F. No physical or mental handicaps

Social worker places client in substance-abuse program.

CLIENT INTAKE

A. White, Jewish, 47 years old

B. Vietnam veteran

C. Suffers from post-traumatic stress disorder

D. Takes many medications

E. Manic-depressive

F. Talks in circles

G. Homeless two months

Social worker recommends Job Connection program.

CLIENT INTAKE

A. White, 60 years old

B. Recently robbed

C. Alcoholic for twenty years

D. Divorced, no family

E. Homeless for two years

F. Formerly lived in the shelter

G. Awaiting a disability check

Social worker recommends two-week stay until the check arrives.

CLIENT INTAKE

A. Native American, 39 years old

B. Alcoholic

C. Just passing through town

D. Recently in a fight; left eye swollen shut

E. Homeless one year

Social worker recommends two-week stay.

tuesday, day 34

After completing another day of teaching on the reservation, I
return to the shelter. It's dinnertime, and I quickly get in line.
Howard falls out of his wheelchair and begins having a seizure. I
freak out because I think he is having a heart attack! Carlos and I
check his pulse and make sure his mouth is clear. Someone hands
me a pillow to place under his head as he continues having violent
convulsions.

Meanwhile, men continue to eat without missing a beat. People
are literally walking over Howard to grab seconds and thirds.
There seems to be no compassion for him. What if it were me, how
would I be treated? The managers take their time phoning for
help, and it seems like an hour before the paramedics show up.
Once they do, even they treat Howard like dirt. I can hear the dis-
dain in their voices. Perhaps he's treated this way because he lives
in a homeless shelter. Is he not a human being? It is not important
that Howard speaks eleven languages fluently. It doesn't matter
that he's dressed in clean clothes or that he attended Penn State.
I'm thinking to myself that these paramedics have no idea how
Howard ended up homeless—nor do they care. They treat him like
an annoying parasite.

I head to the patio after Howard is finally taken away in an ambu-
lance. A client is spreading a rumor that a local soup kitchen has
been placing human waste in its soup. The client also claims to
have found a cockroach in his soup. Every day the soup kitchen
feeds several meals to individuals and families. I've yet to eat at
this place, but if I do, I'll probably skip the soup of the day. The
rumor is probably just a rumor. If it were true, the Health
Department would have closed this place down for sure.

Still, the client's accusations bother me. My biggest concern about living in a shelter is not the threat of violence. It's the threat of TB, hepatitis, illness from food contamination, or any other disease one might contract living in such close proximity with so many in varying states of health.

The shelter has no policies making showers mandatory, washing hands before eating, or screening individuals for contagious diseases other than TB. I take every precaution I can, short of being compulsive. I wash my hands more than is normal. I avoid someone coughing into my face. I use clean towels. I wipe off the toilet seat before I sit on it. I never ask anyone for a drag off their cigarette. I never walk around without shoes on in the barracks or on the patio. Dirty drug needles are found from time to time in the shelter. Using common sense is the best prescription.

wednesday, day 35

Today I will teach high school English. The students are reading a literary masterpiece, *The Great Gatsby* by F. Scott Fitzgerald, a book about a young man and his search for love and success during the Jazz Age. I have another good work day.

Later I return to the shelter, change clothes, and grab something to eat—two hot dogs with lots of mustard, chips, and a cup of punch. After dinner, I find my way to the patio to relax.

A new client is coming on to another client. "Can I give you a blow job?" he asks the man. "Oh yeah," the other man says in disbelief. "If you don't get the hell out of my face, I will kick your ass!" I suspect the gay man will be punched in the mouth if he hangs around another second. As the gay man leaves, the other man calls out, "Faggot!"

Still looking for relaxation, I head to the reading room to record tonight's intakes. But the social worker kicks everyone out. A new client does not want anyone in the room, invoking his right to privacy.

The man acts paranoid about something. I often wonder how many clients are fugitives running from the law. It's easy, I suppose, to hide in any shelter in America and not be noticed. Background checks at this shelter do not exist.

Weapons are hidden all over the place, creating another security hazard. This shelter has no metal detectors in place. On my first night I was asked if I possessed any weapons, and that's all there was to it. Just recently, a client showed me a machete he stashes under his mattress. I asked him why he carries it. "I go nowhere without it," he told me matter-of-factly. I haven't seen any guns in the shelter, though I'm almost certain some find their way in.

The reading room reopens as the new client leaves. I quickly take a seat in the corner. As the social-work intern asks another man the usual line of questions, he begins screaming at her about his troubles. She remains calm, completely unalarmed and not at all intimidated. The man becomes louder, yet she doesn't flinch. I think the man is going to snap any second. But he suddenly becomes quiet. I can't believe it.

Later, Ashley, the intern, tells me with relief, "I was glad someone was in the room." She was terrified by this man but never showed her fear. "Afraid but under control," she says. We talk briefly about the incident, and then our conversation turns to why she does what she does. She is mild-mannered and soft-spoken, with an outwardly caring disposition. Her eyes shine like bright sapphires. She looks out of place here with her fresh-scrubbed, smooth skin and a head full of well-kept brown hair. There is both delicacy and strength in her face.

She tells me about her volunteer work with the homeless and her special interest in working with the mentally ill. She is studying for her master's degree in social work. Ashley has a gift for listening. It takes a special ability to do what she does, and a certain amount of patience and compassion.

People are put on this planet for a reason, and I'm still trying to find my purpose. Ashley has found her purpose.

Meanwhile, men hurry around the shelter, people with a multiplicity of missions—making appointments for tomorrow, signing up for the clothing shed, taking showers, standing in line for medications, asking permission to use the iron, using the pay phone, reading, watching TV, meeting with social workers, filling out job applications, folding clothes, sleeping, or resting their tired feet on their beds from working or walking all day. And the loud speaker squawks incessantly. Midnight, the cat, decides to sleep on my bed. Not in the mood for the intrusion, I gently move her and go to sleep. She heads to the bed of another client; someone will welcome her company.

thursday, day 36

I feel lousy today. I want to stay in bed, but I know I must get ready
for work. My assignment will be first-graders at the primary school
on the reservation. The charter bus stops at the high school, and I
get off with the other primary- and intermediate-grade teachers to
board the twelve-passenger vans. Work with the diminutive ones is
a nice change. First-graders are lovable and innocent. Joy bubbles
up in their laughter and shines in their eyes. Along with the other
teachers I meet my class for the day on the playground. About four
hundred students are running around in what looks like total
chaos. A teacher yells out that it's time to line up.

First-graders make you earn your day's pay without realizing how
hard you've worked. Most educators will agree that working with
primary grades requires hands-on instruction. You are like a
father, a coach, and a teacher, all in one. I hear myself becoming a
broken record, correcting behavior and prodding the kids in the
right direction. One boy will not stay in his seat. I move his desk
next to mine, but he continues to have trouble sitting still. Another
student has a runny nose, and I find myself reminding her repeatedly to wipe her nose but not on her pretty purple dress. The students ask, "Are you married?" "No," I say. "Do you have a girlfriend?" "Yes," I reply. It seems we sing the alphabet song fifty
times before the day is through. We sing nursery rhymes, laugh,
and play. They also work on their handwriting, reading, and math.
The day goes by fast.

After classes are over, I have about an hour to kill before the van
departs. I decide to skip the van and walk to the high school, which
takes about twenty minutes. Beer bottles lie beside the road, hundreds of broken and unbroken bottles. I am reminded of the powerful disease of alcoholism, yet I don't see anyone drinking in pub-

lic. My guess is that drinking happens mostly at night around here. Alcohol is illegal on the reservation. The nearest place to buy booze is in a small town about thirty miles away called Three Points, Arizona. I understand that bootleggers will sell booze to anyone who wants a drink. Seeing the bottles on the ground around the reservation is a reality check.

I arrive at the shelter exhausted. The meal volunteers are late and the men are on edge. Finally the phone rings in the office. The meal team will not make it after all. The shelter has a backup plan and a walk-in cooler stocked with emergency food. Carlos announces over the loudspeaker that we will be fed as soon as possible after something is thrown together. Thirty minutes later the dining room is opened. Tonight's menu: beef stew, sliced bread and butter, fruit cocktail, coffee, and punch.

Later, the compulsive man, with whom I have gained a level of trust, decides to talk to me.

"I entered reform school at age sixteen," he says.

"Really?" I reply.

"Yeah, I was raised in a dysfunctional home." He tells me he was a professional burglar before being caught and sentenced to ten years in prison. He has aspirations of some day doing honest work as a barber.

Another day comes and goes.

friday, day 37

Friday again. This morning on the bus I put on my Walkman head-
set and listen to George Benson. I feel sluggish and sleepy. I tossed
and turned all night. My assignment today is high school French. I
know nothing about the French language, but the lesson plan for
the day has the students watching a travel video on France. I take
roll and introduce myself as Mr. Burns. I inform the students that I
know nothing about French. My whole day is boring as I watch the
movie five times. However, I do come away with a sudden urge to
catch the next plane to Paris. The closest I've been to France is
Naples, Italy, during my navy days. Some of the best pizza I have
ever eaten was in Naples, with a bottle of wine.

Back at the barracks, I change into my shelter attire. Across the
room I hear a new client coughing without end, and it reminds me
of Tom and his wheelchair. This new client is obviously dying a
slow death. He has bronchitis, heart disease, and other maladies
associated with years of smoking. He says he's been this way for
the past seventeen years. At one time he smoked three packs a day.
Today, he pulls an oxygen machine on wheels behind him. On his
bed, I notice he has three cartons of KOOL cigarettes. This guy can
barely breathe as he struggles to make it to the patio. His voice
barks with rasping sounds; his expression is grim as he gazes
across the room.

The meal team shows up tonight. A local church has prepared a
wonderful dinner: spaghetti, French bread, tossed salad, sugar
cookies, and iced tea. The room is full of pleasant activity as we
enjoy our dinner. Then some guy decides to vomit up his food a
few chairs away. I try to continue eating but the food doesn't taste
the same. A few men stop eating, but the majority do not. These
things always seem to happen on Jon's shift.

Today has been busy. I'm able to listen in on four intakes.

CLIENT INTAKE

A. Hispanic, 40 years old

B. Homeless one week

C. His feet are swollen badly, black and blue with frostbite

D. Someone at the VA hospital wants to amputate, but he refuses

Social worker recommends further medical treatment.

CLIENT INTAKE

A. African American, 30 years old

B. Native of Houston, Texas

C. Awaiting a check to arrive

D. Tells social worker little about himself

Social worker offers client a two-week stay.

CLIENT INTAKE

A. White, 23 years old

B. Homeless two weeks, from Ohio

C. Asserts he flew into town and a friend was supposed to meet him at the airport but never showed up; later discovered his friend was arrested on outstanding warrants

D. Non-veteran

E. Heavy drinker

F. Hospitalized for two months for alcohol

G. Collects $615 per month in Social Security benefits

H. Recently tried to commit suicide by taking one hundred doses of LSD

Social worker recommends alcohol-treatment program.

CLIENT INTAKE

A. African-American, 58 years old

B. From Texas

C. Suffers back problems

D. Walks with a cane

E. Heroin addict

F. Awaiting a benefits check

Social worker recommends two-week stay.

I think about myself, how I've changed since my stay at the shelter began. It's been thirty-six days since I've had a drink or drug. I can't believe it.

saturday, day 38

No work today. Last night I agreed to clean the restroom. After breakfast, I don my plastic gloves and load up with the many disinfectants available for this dreadful but necessary chore. I much prefer cleaning the office, but last night I was late to sign the cleanup list.

As on all weekends, the concern I have is with what to do. First, I return some library books. As I enter the library, I see the man who tried to sell me the Walkman on the pay phone. He no longer lives in the shelter. Last night he was passed out on the shelter's front doorstep. As I pass the phones to catch the elevator to the third floor, I overhear him telling someone he needs money right away. His face looks as if he was in a fight. The clothes on his back are dirty, blackened and greasy like a garage mechanic's. His hair is matted with grime.

I stop at the periodicals section and begin reading out-of-state newspapers, but I can't seem to concentrate—my mind races. I feel impatient and restless; as soon as possible, I want to be back on my feet and not living this way. I look out the window at people down below. The weather is slightly overcast, and the sun tries to burn through the clouds. Inside, I notice several homeless men idly sitting and resting beside their bedrolls. A library security guard passes by every ten minutes on her rounds. I decide to leave the library and catch a bus back to the shelter.

My laundry bag is sitting on top of my bed, so I start to fold my clothes. I notice that not all of them have been washed. Another man has taken over the job from Sal, who entered substance-abuse treatment a few days ago. I confront the new guy about my dirty clothes, which are mixed up with my clean clothes. He tells me some of my articles were not properly tagged. I remember doing it right, but I just shake my head and walk away, thinking this guy must have a light bulb randomly flickering on and off inside his head. Good help is hard to find around here. The only reason this guy got the job is because he did it several years ago as a client.

What I need right now is a little humor, and I find it, lo and behold, in the restroom of all places. I'm standing over a urinal taking care of my bladder when I notice a sign in front of my face. It reads: "Would all of you ballplayers with short bats please stand closer to home plate. Thank you. Staff."

For a Saturday, it has been typical. Relax and take it easy. The rest of the evening is spent reading on my bed.

sunday, day 39

A young client is choking another for jumping in front of him in the breakfast line. The fight is quickly broken up by a third man. I cannot believe what's just taken place for a bowl of cereal. I would understand it if only one bowl were left and it wasn't some generic brand.

I iron a shirt to wear to church. The shelter iron leaks brown stuff onto my clean, blue dress shirt, which now has spots all over. Two of my shirts came back dirty from the new laundry man. Frustrated, now I must go to church in a polo shirt. Church not only offers me spiritual fuel, but it is a time to forget about my burdens for a few hours. It's a joyous time for me. Today's Palm Sunday sermon focuses on "Despair and Hope." I leave church spiritually recharged, ready to take on another week.

Entering the shelter after church uses up some of my spiritual fuel right away. I see hopelessness and helplessness, despair and idleness. I keep telling myself, soon I will move on to a better life.

Another client is being asked to leave for not following shelter rules. I've noticed this eighteen-year-old's odd behavior for the past three days. He gives people the finger for no reason. He's confrontational with others. Today he stuck his hand in another man's back pocket and was nearly choked to death. In three days he's driven everyone mad, and he has to go.

Shortly after dinner, the compulsive man finds a bottle containing urine on his bunk. Someone has played a joke on him. He hits the roof! His lips pucker with annoyance. For the next hour he's in the restroom washing his hands to rid himself of any germs from handling the bottle of urine.

The man with the oxygen machine asks a manager to dial 911. He's having trouble breathing, he says, coughing uncontrollably. The paramedics arrive and begin taking his vital signs. They also connect him to a heart monitor, and quickly whisk him away to the VA hospital.

Tonight on the patio a young client brags to another about how much money he makes holding his sign on street corners. His sign reads: "Homeless, Hungry, God Bless." On a good day he says he can make $20. "I make $560 per month from Social Security." he says. I see homeless people all over Tucson holding signs. Some of the signs are funny, in a way. "Why Lie? I Need a Beer." One man's sign reads: "Dog Needs Dog Food and I Need a Job." A lot of homeless people hold signs to support their drinking or drug habits, but perhaps a few really need the help.

The balance between church and shelter leaves me between hope and despair. Sometimes I think without a spiritual equilibrium I couldn't stand this madness. I must pray every day. It's the only thing that keeps me going.

monday, day 40

Monday blues. The 100-mile-round-trip bus ride each day takes its toll on me. Today I will work at the primary school in physical education. The lesson plans call for the children to do stretching exercises and play kickball. The kindergartners are to work on their agility skills. I'm instructed to divide each class into teams. I hastily construct a makeshift obstacle course, made of several Earth balls, hula hoops, bean bags, and jump ropes. I tell the students what to do. Each one will run the course and then tag the next person in line. Boys and girls are stumbling over their shoelaces. Some are falling down. It is a sight to see these little kids having just plain old competitive fun for thirty minutes.

Each Monday, Ivan meets with those of us who are in Job Connection. To date I have saved $800 in my account after six weeks. Despite my success so far, meeting with Ivan leaves a bad taste in my mouth. I ask him for $10 of my money to buy more bus tickets, and he begins to question me as if in a police interrogation. He makes me furious, giving me what amounts to a lecture about how to spend my money and treating me in a demeaning way. He's on some power trip. I realize some men in the program spend their money as fast as they make it, but this is a first for me to take from my savings, and I need the bus tickets to get to work. Also, I have more money saved than anyone else in the program. I've followed the rules to the dotted line, and he gives me static about how other people in the program have screwed up. I'm feeling insulted. He acts like I'm at his mercy, and I suppose I am.

In the end, he gives me my $10, but I'm so offended I feel like moving out. I have the feeling that Ivan wants me to fail. He's been known to kick guys out of the program for breathing the wrong way. I've been busting my butt catching three buses to work at 5:00

A.M., and this guy gives me a hard time about $10.

The steam on my forehead slowly evaporates, and I try to remain civil-minded. A few minutes later I start a conversation with a client named Marvin, who tells me a story about his passion for riding freight trains across the country. His most recent journey included riding a train from San Francisco to Tucson.

"How do you eat?" I ask.

"I eat in soup kitchens and panhandle from people wherever I happen to be," he says.

"How long have you been riding trains?"

"Three years."

"Do you ever worry about injuring yourself?"

"All the time," he admits.

"What makes you want to ride freight trains?"

"I lost my job at a steel mill in Pittsburgh, and it's something I have always wanted to do," he says softly. Someday he hopes to tell train stories to his grandchildren.

Overall, my day has been good. I've worked an honest day, I've had fun with children, and I didn't drink or use drugs. Reminding myself of my past on a daily basis keeps me grounded. Tomorrow is a new day, and only God knows what's ahead for me.

tuesday, day 41

I leave for work at 5:00 A.M. but return to town early. When I board a bus to the university library, I recognize a man who lives in the shelter sitting in the back. I take a seat near him. The man is Hispanic, around forty years old, and he introduces himself as Smooth. I tell him my name and we make small talk. Smooth tells me about his prison time in Folsom for drug trafficking. Tattoos cover both of his arms.

"I only went to two years in high school before I quit. Man, I wasted fifteen years of my fucking life doing stupid shit," he says with dazed exasperation. "What do you do?" he asks.

"I substitute teach," I reply.

"Don't you have to go to college for that shit?" he asks.

"Yes," I answer. "Take care, dude, this is my stop." I get off the bus, taken with the thought that Smooth and I live in the same place. I sometimes wonder how my life would have been had I gone to prison. Smooth reminds me of a younger brother of mine who spent the majority of his life in prison. He never completed high school. My brother was a great example of a rebel without a cause. He died from a gunshot wound to his chest when he was twenty-eight years old.

I've seen uncles and other relatives in and out of prison. Self-empowerment and a determined attitude made me not want to end up like so many of my relatives. By the same token, living in a homeless shelter doesn't make me a much better person.

Growing up in south Phoenix was not always easy for me. Fighting to defend myself was almost a daily occurrence, except that then we fought with fists, not guns. Kids in my neighborhood stole bikes, not cars. Families got along for the most part. Now people are lucky to know their next-door neighbors.

My parents supplied my brothers and sisters and me with the basics, such as food and shelter, yet they lacked good parenting skills. Being in a dysfunctional family means you take with you lots of emotional baggage. I saw my stepfather beat my mother countless times. I was slapped and kicked around like a rag doll. This sort of abuse hurts a kid, and the hurt continues even today. Besides the physical abuse, substance abuse was also a regular part of my home life. As a teenager I saw my stepfather shoot heroin in his arm many times. Empty beer and liquor bottles were part of the furniture in our house.

Living at home felt a lot like walking on egg shells. Between the constant drunkenness, fighting, and emotional and physical abuse, I sought help from teachers or anyone who would listen. A coach was able to help raise enough money for me to attend a summer youth basketball camp, and I later became a Phoenix Suns ball boy. I worked in the visiting-team locker room. I saw some of the greatest players ever—Pete Maravich, Willis Reed, Connie Hawkins, Jerry West, JoJo White, John Havlicek, Oscar Robertson, Walt Frazier, Nate Archibald, and other great stars of the 1970s. Friends in my neighborhood envied me. I felt special, which I never felt at home. A child without parental love is like a chick left in the nest by a mother bird who flies away and never returns.

I thought, then, like many inner-city kids think today, that basketball or some kind of professional sport would be my ticket out of ghetto life. Working with the Suns organization made me realize that the way out was through education, not spending hours at the city park playing basketball. I realized not everyone can be good enough to make the pros. If I knew then what I know now, I would have taken my education more seriously earlier on.

wednesday, day 42, last day

Today I say good-bye. I'm scared, but at the same time thrilled to be leaving. I've met some good people at the shelter, but now it's time to move on with my life. I feel I have accomplished much and learned from this experience. Having resilience has definitely helped to end my homelessness. My savings account has reached $900—not a lot of money, but a good start.

I've found a small efficiency apartment in downtown Tucson, where the rent will be $250 a month, including utilities. After running some errands, I return to gather my belongings at the shelter for the last time. On my way out I see Maury. He is a man I have come to like. He can't believe I'm actually leaving today. Carlos and a social worker wish me well. It's ironic that I arrived in a cab and depart the same way. But now my self-esteem is much higher.

I'll no longer have to wait in line for showers or toilets. I'm going to have my own private bathroom. I'll no longer have to wait in line to eat. Nor will I have to wake up at 5:00 A.M. to make sure my laundry is in on time to be washed. No more worry about some guy next to me who smells and snores in his sleep. The only odors in my apartment will be mine. Finally, no more loudspeaker interrupting my thoughts. And I can sleep late without any disturbances; no timetable to get out the door in the morning.

I realize that rules serve a purpose in any institution, and the shelter is no different. And I'm aware of what I now have to do, what rules of my own I must follow to succeed. One, keep my head screwed on right. Two, be responsible. And never forget what I have gone through for the past forty-one days.

My new apartment is in a large, two-story, rustic brick house, which has been converted into nine one-room efficiency apartments. The house sits on Stone Avenue, across the street from the Tucson Police Department. Next to the house sits a shady, run-down motel with rooms rented by the week to people who have spent every cent of their last paycheck.

I have access to a second-floor balcony, where the view is picturesque. I can see a beautiful downtown skyline, and also the massive Santa Catalina Mountains to the north. The 210-square-foot room is clean and equipped with a small evaporative cooler, hanging off the window ledge and about to give out. Two antique chairs sit in corners of the room, giving the place a homey quality. The wooden floor was once varnished, but has now been painted over with bright russet-red paint. I fall in love with the place immediately.

The bathroom was built in 1909. The toilet and sink look just as old. My bed sleeps two. A wheel on the frame under the box spring is missing, so I find a brick under the sink and place it beneath to make the bed level temporarily. My stove is a two-burner hot plate, and a few dishes are left from the person who lived here before. I make a short list of cooking supplies I plan to buy.

I unpack my "Samsonite"—garbage bags of clothes. Then I step outside on the balcony, look at cars passing by, and take in the fresh air.

I treat myself to a night on the town. I walk the dark streets of Tucson until I come across the Cushing Street Bar and Grill, once noted for having some of the best steaks in town. Tonight they also have a jazz band playing. After dinner, I have an urge for an ice cold beer. It's been forty days since I last had a drink. The waiter brings a cold beer. I drink it and feel like I have just committed a crime. A wave of apprehension sweeps through me. One lousy beer. Forty days wasted. Deep down I know the consequences of my drinking. It is a fast highway to Malfunction Junction and God knows what else.

My first night in the room alone feels strange. Without a TV or radio, a deadly silence fills the room, and I can hear every sound outside as the sun sets. I seem to be waiting for a loudspeaker to blast at any minute or for Jon to knock on the door telling me to turn off the lights. It finally hits me that this is what I have been working toward. I must now live on my own without the routines, rules, or help of the shelter.

I realize it will not be easy as I rejoin the real world—working an honest job, paying my bills, and staying off the booze and drugs. Success also means being honest with myself and others who care about me. My emotions run high as I wonder what's going to happen next. Will I ever come to terms with my disease and get the help I desperately need? Have I really learned my lesson living in the shelter? What chance have I got, based on my past drinking and drugging?

The choices I make from this day on will determine my fate.

epilogue

After being out of the shelter for six months, I return as an outsider. My purpose is to remind me of my homeless past.

A few days before, I settled a small insurance claim for my back injury and bought a used 1980 two-door Honda Accord. No more buses. With school out for the summer, I have landed a summer job with the Parks Department working in recreation. I pull up in front of the shelter just as church volunteers are loading up their cars after serving dinner. The patio looks the same: clients mill about smoking cigarettes while others play cards and dominoes.

As I get out of my car and make my way to the front door, I feel all eyes are on me. I ring the bell. I look over into the patio yard and see myself in their shoes not long ago. Carlos opens the door and lets me in.

Midnight the cat hurries out, jumps up, and leaves dirty paw prints on my car, which I just washed. Sleeping on my bed was not enough, she has to rest atop my clean car. This is the welcome I get. If it weren't for the nostalgia, I'd be outraged.

Carlos is still here, but there are also new faces among the managers. High turnover is common. People come and go.

Tonight the barracks is overflowing. Managers scurry about, fielding questions from clients, working the front desk, answering the phones, monitoring the grounds, passing out medications, and closing down the patio because the next day's cleanup list hasn't been filled out. Men often avoid placing their names on the list—until a strong urge to light up a cigarette comes on and they find the patio closed.

I see a familiar face from when I lived here, a man who was a shelter manager on the night shift. I never took the time to get to know him; I was always sleeping during his shift. All managers were once clients themselves. What better people to help run a shelter than those who have been homeless.

I begin another conversation with a client about his chronic unemployment woes. He shows me his résumé to prove he has a master's degree in business administration. He comes across confident, yet cocky. I see a glimmer of hope in his eyes. He looks determined to get back on his feet. He seems sure of himself and his rightful place in the universe. Other men appear down and out, with dim hope. I see men in despair, drunks, addicts, the mentally ill, the broken-hearted, the sick, the powerless, the ashamed, and the lonely.

My visit is a reality check, seeing homelessness from the outside looking in. It also gives me a moment to listen, watch, learn, and to be reminded that the men's home used to be mine.

Since leaving the shelter I have occasionally run across former clients that I knew when I stayed there, or I have heard about them through the grapevine.

Maury the salesman. While driving my car one day, I recognize Maury waiting for a city bus. I immediately make a U-turn to offer him a ride. We have coffee and catch up on old times. His appearance hasn't changed. He's wearing a tweed jacket and hat, bifocals, and a neatly trimmed gray beard. He remains funny and good-natured. He also continues to repair vacuum cleaners and sewing machines. After coffee, I drop him off at a house where he rents a guest room.

Sal. After successfully completing the VA drug-treatment program in Tucson, Sal moved into a halfway house. He had worked as a pharmacist before he ended up in the shelter, and now he holds down a job at the VA hospital, where I occasionally see him when I have business there. We joke about the time a client stole his socks.

The compulsive man. One day I run into him near the Greyhound bus terminal, with his backpack loaded down like a crammed U-Haul trailer. At first glance, I notice everything about him is still exceptionally clean from head to toe. It appears that he remains homeless, unemployed, and living the best way he knows how.

Mohammed. I occasionally see Mohammed around town. After leaving the shelter, he entered a drug treatment program at the VA hospital. Word has it he relapsed with only two weeks left in the program. He says he is unemployed and sleeps with old friends in areas of town known for heavy drug activities.

Lamar. He lived briefly in the shelter's transitional housing while working as a painter covering over graffiti in the city. He attended months of AA meetings and even joined a church. The last I heard he quit his job and moved back to North Carolina. Weeks earlier, we had talked about his homesickness.

James. After leaving the shelter, I didn't see James for quite some time. Then I saw him walking downtown wearing a new baseball cap, a bright new orange starter's jacket, white sweatpants, and a brand new pair of $150 tennis shoes. Missing is an upper front tooth, which he doesn't care to talk about. He looks healthy and not drunk or on drugs. He says he no longer breaks into parking garages with his special tweezers. He's unemployed, yet from his front pocket he pulls out a thick roll of bills. His residence these days is in and out of shelters, he says.

Ivan. He is no longer affiliated with Primavera. I stayed in contact with him after I left the shelter, playing basketball with him and other staff members at a local park. He currently works in management for a personnel firm. He is happily married, with two boys and two girls.

Midnight and Rambo. Both felines are alive and well! They continue to live at the shelter without a worry in the world. If only they could speak and share their stories about the many men they've seen come and go, what stories they would be!

Me. A year after leaving the shelter my life went wayward again. Living alone in an apartment building occupied by other alcoholics didn't help. Even the apartment manager was drinking all of the time. The man next door had blackouts so bad, he couldn't remember what he had said or done the day before. He had flashbacks from Vietnam and conversations with imaginary people. When he was drunk, you could hear him in his apartment kicking walls and doors and throwing chairs. This guy scared the shit out of me. A prostitute moved in across the hall. Her door opened and closed in the wee hours of the morning. After she moved in, the cops were there almost every day. Another tenant and his girlfriend were continually fighting. They both ended up going to jail several times but always made up. A block away was a liquor store, which became my home away from home.

I had what most homeless people dream of—an apartment, a car, a job, and a bank account. Yet I became powerless over drinking. My days and nights became a cycle of living in a constant state of drunkenness and in total isolation. I went to work with hangovers and went to bed drunk or stoned, sometimes both.

Despite my experience drying out and living in the shelter, once again I fell off the wagon. I was out of control. My bills began piling up. I was back riding the city buses because I didn't have the money to get my car fixed. I would buy beer and let the bottles pile up inside my apartment just so no one would see them outside and know I had a problem. I'd cook and let the dishes stack up until they became moldy.

Often I bought food and discovered I didn't have enough money for booze or drugs. Then I would take the food back to get a refund so I could buy more booze. Often I didn't have any food to eat, so I would go to soup kitchens. I'd lie that I had small children so I could get enough food for two or three days.

Going to work became irregular. The teachers and students noticed a difference in my behavior. I kept to myself and stopped interacting with anyone at school. I'd call in sick or not call in at all. Sometimes I'd make up some lie about why I wasn't there. I even hocked my TV to buy booze and drugs. On pay day, I would get the TV out, then do it all over again when I needed cash. I can't recall how many times I faced eviction notices. My health and mind were in bad shape. I stopped going to church. I hated myself each day I woke up.

Something had to be done if I was to get this gorilla off my back.

I tried unsuccessfully on my own to battle this disease, and I ended up like so many others who have tried to quit on their own. My disease has caused me anguish and hopelessness. One morning I woke up and decided I needed professional help. The empty beer bottles piled in my apartment from the night before were a clear message. Enough was enough. I checked myself into the VA hospital and got set up for treatment. At this point I thought I was crazy. Within days I was admitted into the outpatient chemical-dependency treatment program.

During treatment I began to realize what I was really up against with my disease. The four-month program included intense group therapy, which I desperately needed. For the first time in my life I stopped lying to myself. In treatment, I was taught how to live a life away from booze and drugs, how to live a healthy lifestyle, and that I must have the willingness to do the footwork.

Treatment has made me more aware of my feelings. I learned about relapse prevention and warning signs, about the importance of honesty with myself and others. Each day now when I wake up I pray to God to give me the courage to live another day sober. I gave up my apartment and moved into the oldest halfway house in Tucson for alcoholic recovery. Residents sleep in a dormitory-style building, with semi-private rooms. Twenty-four men live in the house, including a house manager, an assistant manager, a kitchen manager/ weekday cook, and a weekend cook. The house has been in the business of helping drunks and addicts since the 1960s. Residents pay rent, which covers their food. Shortly after I moved in I was hired as the weekend cook, making it possible for me to teach during the week.

The house runs a small bingo hall two days a week to raise funds for food. The players are all ages—all coming for the chance win a $1,000 jackpot. One woman who plays, rain or shine, is eighty-nine years old.

Living around sober people is critical to my sobriety—no question about that! Since living in this home, I have bonded with others who have decided to live sober and die sober. In my brief recovering period of three years, I have seen friends falter. On the other hand, I have known friends who are making the most of their recovery. One man has lived here for 18 years.

Does it get better when the booze and drugs are gone? You bet! I have been promoted to assistant manager, with a small salary, health insurance, a private room, and the keys to the refrigerator. Today my priorities are: God, AA, and me.

However, the person with twenty years of sobriety has just as much chance of relapsing as the person who has two months. Once a drunk, always a drunk. For me, I take it one day at a time. Today my life is simple. Today my life is about honesty. I have a singleness of purpose: to stay sober. The fellowship of AA and other support groups, which I lean on, have given me the encouragement and strength to remain sober. These are the tools I continue to use in my daily life. The most important thing, though, is that I must continue to have a willingness to stay sober.

This means I must do the footwork, listen, and learn from those who have a significant amount of sobriety under their belts. However, no support group can save me. No individual can save me. I can only save myself with the help of a higher power, which I choose to call God.

I never want to end up in another shelter. Like all drunks and addicts, in sobriety I will always have it in me to take another drink or use another drug. My story is not unique. Helping those who suffer the disease of alcoholism or drug abuse will always be a challenge.

My experience of living in a shelter will never be forgotten. The homeless in our society continue to suffer in a land rich with resources. Advocacy remains the strongest weapon in the fight. My volunteerism may not end homelessness, but it helps. I remain two paychecks away from being homeless again. Moreover, more and more Americans face this reality. Each day in this country men, women, and children are turned away from shelters for lack of space. I was lucky. Next time, maybe not.

ABOUT THE AUTHOR

Bobby Burns's book *Shelter: One Man's Journey from Homelessness to Hope* is the true story about his life living in a Tucson homeless shelter in the 1990s. A chapter from this book has been adopted in a 2008 college textbook. Bobby once served on the board of the Primavera Foundation, a homeless advocacy group in Tucson.

Shelter has been featured in *Publishers Weekly*, the *Chicago Sun-Times*, the *San Diego Tribune*, and the *Arizona Republic*, among other publications. He has published poems in the *Louisiana Review, Sandscripts Magazine*, and *City Life* newspaper and has completed an unpublished book of poetry. In 2008 he studied poetry under poet Steve Kowit at a Pima Community College poetry writing workshop.

While an academic advisor at Louisiana State University at Eunice in 2005, he interviewed famed novelist Ernest Gaines at his plantation home in New Roads, Louisiana. The interview was published in *Oxford Magazine* in 2006.

Burns writes for the *Arizona Informant Newspaper*, a weekly African American newspaper, and is a former columnist with the *Tucson Citizen* newspaper. He's also co-hosts the "On the Bookshelf" radio show about writers. He earned an M.A. from Northern Arizona University and a B.A. degree from Arizona State University. He recently celebrated 14 years clean and sober.